Survival Kit
for Youth

A Practical Guide to Spiritual Growth
by Ralph W. Neighbour, Jr.

LifeWay Press
Nashville, Tennessee

ISBN 0-8054-9602-5

This book is a resource in Personal Life category of the
Christian Growth Study Plan.
Course CG-0410
Dewey Decimal Classification: 248.4
Subject: Heading: CHRISTIAN LIFE \\ SALVATION

The Scripture quotations marked NASB are from the *New American Standard Bible.* Copyright © The
Lockman Foundation, 1960, 1962, 1963, 1971, 1972, 1973, 1975. Used by permission.

The Scripture quotations marked RSV are from the *Revised Standard Version
of the Bible,* copyrighted 1946, 1952, © 1971, 1973.

The Scripture quotations marked (TEV) are from the *Today's English Version,* Second Edition Copyright ©
1966, 1971, 1976, 1992 American Bible Society.
Used by permission.

Printed in the United States of America.

Student Ministry Publishing
LifeWay Church Resources
One LifeWay Plaza
Nashville, TN 37234-0174

To order additional copies of this resource: WRITE LifeWay Church Resources Customer Service,
One LifeWay Plaza, Nashville, TN 37234-0113; FAX (615)251-5933; PHONE 1-800-458-2772;
E-MAIL to Customer Service@lifeway.com; ONLINE at www.lifeway.com;
or visit the LifeWay Christian Store serving you.

We believe that the Bible has God for its author; salvation for its end; and truth, without any
mixture of error, for its matter and that all Scripture is totally true and trustworthy. The 2000
statement of *The Baptist Faith and Message* is our doctrinal guideline.

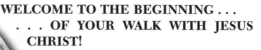

WELCOME TO THE BEGINNING . . .
. . . OF YOUR WALK WITH JESUS CHRIST!

You have made life's most important decision. You have given your life to Jesus Christ. Your commitment is based on your faith that He is the Son of God; that He has the power to be your Lord.

This book is called SURVIVAL KIT FOR YOUTH. It has been written for you by those who have been where you are. Please don't misunderstand the term *SURVIVAL*. It does not imply that you may lose your relationship to Jesus Christ. About those who trust Him He said: "I give eternal life to them, and they shall never perish; and no one shall snatch them out of My hand" (John 10:28, NASB). Instead, "SURVIVAL" refers to your ability to function as a new Christian, growing spiritually and living victoriously. The purpose of this book is to help you begin right now to put into action your decision to make Christ your Savior and your Lord.

Certain truths are implied in such a lifetime decision. Your faith in Christ's lordship is based on the facts . . .

  . . . that before now you have lived for yourself;
  . . . that God did not create you to live in such a manner;
  . . . that God has a greater purpose for your life;
  . . . and that you will find that greater purpose for your life only by making Jesus Christ Lord of all you are.

Think back to your conversion . . .

Perhaps you thought a great deal about Christ's death on the cross. Your past years of trying to do God's job—choosing right and wrong for yourself—may have bothered you. How could you ever face God? The purpose of Christ's suffering was to make it possible for you to be forgiven and to have an open relationship with God.

You prayed, confessing your sin and need for God. You knew God's forgiveness in that moment. You welcomed Christ's control as you turned away from your old values and your old lifestyle.

As you prayed, you were reborn! In your first birth, you were placed in a physical world. In this new birth, you were placed in a spiritual world. New values and a new lifestyle awaited you. It was all brand new, wasn't it? The joy, the exhilaration . . . like suddenly coming from death to life!

Now . . .
You want to let Jesus be Lord. The problem is, there are so many things you want to **know.** You are like any new baby: you have **life;** now, you want **nourishment** so that you may grow. There are many biblical truths you need to "feed on," right at the start.

First . . .
Set apart a **definite time** and **place** to meet your Lord **daily.** This is a matter of discipline. Without it, you will not grow spiritually as you should. Call it your "Quiet Time." Do not delay. BEGIN AT ONCE. The location should be the same each day; the time also should be as regular as your schedule permits. To help you, the first week of your SURVIVAL KIT will give you practical pointers for a lifetime of Quiet Times. Also, the whole book is written to provide you with five daily Quiet Times each week. Make the use of it a constant habit.

For this reason, you are urged **not** to do more than one day's work in this book at a time. **Remember:** The material has been written to develop new habits in your life. These new patterns of life with Christ in control will take time to develop. As they do, you will feel pulled between your old habits and your new ones. It's normal. All of us have experienced it. Old patterns of thinking and acting will be clashing constantly with new ones. Old habits will be confronted with the demands of Christ. Your daily Quiet Time will become the **first new habit** of your Christian life.

There are years of truths you may learn, but **five** are **critical** for your immediate survival. You will become acquainted with them next.

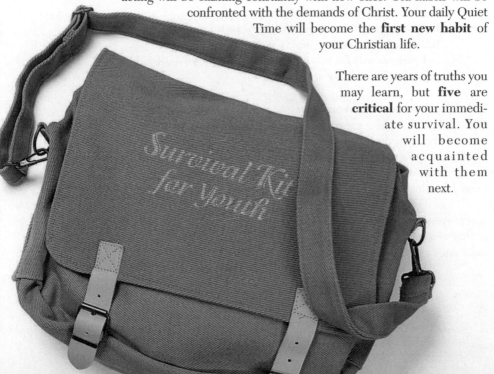

WHAT'S IN YOUR SURVIVAL KIT?

THE CONTENTS OF YOUR SURVIVAL KIT CAN BE PUT ON THE FINGERS OF ONE HAND . . . Your hand can help you remember the five truths you will be learning.

The **thumb** works in cooperation with each **finger.** The first truth you will learn has a working relationship with each of the other four. You always must **combine** the first truth with the rest to **survive** as a Christian.

The materials you will study are designed to help you understand how God works in your life and in your world. In addition, when you have finished, you will be able to explain to your non-Christian friends many important facts about your new faith.

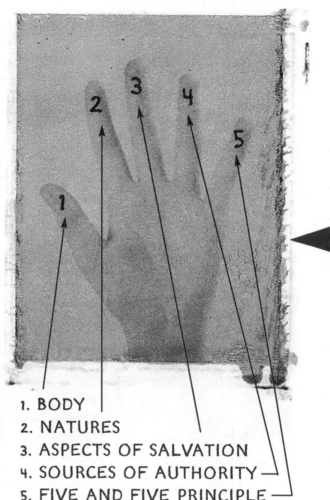

1. BODY
2. NATURES
3. ASPECTS OF SALVATION
4. SOURCES OF AUTHORITY
5. FIVE AND FIVE PRINCIPLE

You face many problems and temptations daily. Your SURVIVAL KIT has been written to guide you through the ones faced by most new believers. But remember . . . what you will learn is only a **foundation** for your new life. A great number of **floors** will be built upon it in the years to come, as you grow in Bible understanding, as you develop discipleship skills, and as you learn to participate in the missions outreach of your church. This will happen as you participate actively in the Bible study, the training, and the missions organizations in your church.

NEARLY ALL NEW CHRISTIANS GO THROUGH THE FOLLOWING STAGES.

1. THE EXCITEMENT STAGE

As a new Christian, you are aware that Jesus Christ has come literally to live in your life. The life you now live is new! Naturally, you will want to share this new life with your unbelieving friends. This is a happy stage!

During this excitement stage the most important single fact for you to learn is that you are now a part of the body of Christ, the church. Placing you in that body is one of the first works of the Holy Spirit. Being baptized in water is your public witness to the fact. In being baptized, you are telling the whole world that you have become new and that your life now belongs to the Lord Jesus Christ.

If you think only about your own personal relationship to Christ, you will miss a great truth: YOUR CHRISTIAN GROWTH DEPENDS STRONGLY ON YOUR RELATIONSHIP TO THE BODY OF CHRIST, THE CHURCH. Read 1 Corinthians 11:29-30.

2. THE FIGHT STAGE

Perhaps you have boasted to a few of your unbelieving friends of your new victory over sin. It's true that such a victory is real in your life, but things are not always smooth. Temper and frustration return. Resentment creeps in . . . along with jealousy, criticism, and gossip. You discover you still have these old habits bothering you.

Now you face the danger of acting the part of a victorious Christian. You think: I'll just cover this up. I'll "fake" a joy I do not now have. You become busy at church, thinking that going to all youth activities will help. After a while you can no longer fool yourself; you have started to live a lie. You have no inner victory. You are defeated. You feel like a hypocrite. You have become a defeated Christian.

Before that happens—before the fight stage begins—you must be introduced to an important truth: When the new nature of Christ entered your life, the old nature did not die. You now possess two natures, not one.

3. THE DOUBTING STAGE

If not taught properly, many new Christians will enter a doubting stage. They wrongly feel their salvation is a finished thing, received at the moment they received Christ. In one sense, this is absolutely true: ALL CHRIST HAS TO GIVE YOU WAS PROVIDED IN THAT MOMENT WHEN YOU BECAME A CHRISTIAN. But it's like receiving a new pocket calculator as a gift. It's complete when it comes to you, but you must understand it to get the greatest benefit from it.

Jesus promised that when you became a Christian, the Holy Spirit would enter you as a teacher and would teach you all things (John 14:26). As the inner war between the new nature and the old nature takes place, you begin to feel a need for more information about your salvation. You desire more truth! You must learn that your salvation has three aspects: it is a point in time, when Christ enters; a process of time, as the power of the new nature gives you constant victory over the old nature; a final point in time, when Christ will set you free forever from the presence of the old nature.

4. THE PANIC-SEARCH-FOR-TRUTH STAGE

To spare you from this stage, you will study next the true source of Christian truth and compare it to three other sources.

One person you talk to may suggest that you reason out the questions about your new faith. Another may tell you about a big experience that the Lord will give you, which will solve all your problems. Still another friend may recommend the traditions of the church and may suggest they hold the solutions to your questions.

The first person builds faith on intellect; the second person, on experience; and the third person rests all beliefs on tradition. You will learn that, although all three of these sources of authority have a certain place, the true source of authority for a Christian is the written Word of God, the Bible.

5. THE "SILENT CHRISTIAN" STAGE

Have you already met some "silent Christians" who never witness? If you haven't, you will! You may wonder why they are that way. Perhaps these insights will help you understand them:

1. They feel that other Christians who know more and doubt less should be the ones to witness.

2. They do not want to brag about things they are unsure of or give a false impression of victorious Christian living.

3. In place of faith sharing, they work hard in church activities that do not require any witness to non-Christians.

MANY CHRISTIANS SLEEP IN THIS "SILENT CHRISTIAN" STAGE!

Christians who do not witness verbally may be busy in the church, but it is not likely that their lives will influence many other persons to become Christians. Before that happens to YOU, resolve to study the final section of this book. Learn about the **Five-and-Five Principle.**

On the Journey with Your Survival Kit

This chart shows how the 11-week devotional plan of the Survival Kit will prepare you for the various stages of Christian growth. Write in the dates you will begin each five-day Quiet Time. Begin on Monday. Use Saturday and Sunday Quiet Time to prepare for Sunday School and Discipleship Training. Color the diamond after you have completed each week's study.

Week/Date	Subject	Stage
◇ 1 _____	The Indwelling Christ	Excitement
◇ 2 _____	One Body—Its Life	
◇ 3 _____	One Body—Its Service	
◇ 4 _____	Two Natures—The New Nature	Fight
◇ 5 _____	Two Natures—The Old Nature	
◇ 6 _____	Three Aspects of Salvation—Its Beginning and Completion	Doubting
◇ 7 _____	Three Aspects of Salvation—A Daily Process	
◇ 8 _____	Four Sources of Authority—Three Inadequate Sources	Panic-Search-for-truth
◇ 9 _____	Four Sources of Authority—One True Source	
◇ 10 _____	The Five-and-Five Principle—Five You Can Win by Prayer	"Silent Christian"
◇ 11 _____	The Five-and-Five Principle—Five You Can Win by Witnessing	

Scripture Memory Verses

Check the box when you have memorized the Scripture for the week.

❑ Psalm 119:11	Week 1	❑ Romans 5:10	Week 7
❑ Romans 12:4-5	Week 2	❑ 1 Corinthians 2:14	Week 8
❑ 1 Peter 4:10	Week 3	❑ 2 Timothy 3:16	Week 9
❑ Galatians 5:22-23	Week 4	❑ Philippians 4:6	Week 10
❑ Colossians 3:8-10	Week 5	❑ Matthew 28:18-20	Week 11
❑ Philippians 1:6	Week 6		

Would you expect to be healthy if the only time you ate a meal was on Sunday morning? Of course not! You would not survive long. Do you think you will be any healthier **spiritually** if you wait until Sunday morning to digest spiritual truth?

A **daily Quiet Time** provides regular contact with your source of spiritual life, Jesus Christ Himself. Each day, you simply **must** find a time to be alone with Christ! Here are some suggestions.

1. HAVE A SPECIFIC TIME AND PLACE. A desk, a table, or even the side of your bed will do. It is important that you schedule 10 minutes for your Quiet Time. If possible, schedule your Quiet Time at the start of your day.

2. BE CONSISTENT. A hit-and-miss pattern is an indication that you are not as serious as you need to be about growing as a Christian. Your Quiet Time is when you "program" your day to let Christ be Lord of your life.

3. HAVE A BIBLE AND A PENCIL HANDY. For the first 11 weeks of your Quiet Time, you will be using the SURVIVAL KIT five days a week. Use your Sunday School lesson and your Discipleship Training material on the other two days each week. Later, you will want to use a small notebook for keeping a spiritual growth diary.

4. BEGIN WITH PRAYER. Open your heart to Christ, offering Him the right to teach, to discipline, or to direct you as you study. Tell Him you love Him. Share your concerns with Him.

5. END WITH A DEFINITE PROJECT FOR THE DAY, RELATED TO WHAT YOU HAVE LEARNED. Before you stop, decide how you can live out the truth you have learned in your Quiet Time.

HAVE TODAY'S QUIET TIME RIGHT NOW . . .

PRAY: Express your love for God. Thank Him for giving you His life through Christ. Share with Him the special ways you need His power in your life. Ask Him to live through you as you live your life today.

By this we know that we abide in Him and He in us, because He has given us of His Spirit. And we have beheld and bear witness that the Father has sent the Son to be the Savior of the world. Whoever confesses that Jesus is the Son of God, God abides in him, and he in God.
—1 John 4:13-15, NASB

As you read the Bible, God's Word, you're getting spiritual nourishment. But are you "digesting" what you read? One way to help you "digest" the thoughts in Scripture verses is to rewrite them in your own words. *Try doing this now, with the verses you have just read.*

According to these verses, what gift confirms that you have become a Christian?

As a Christian you have received God's gift of His Holy Spirit. What confession causes God to abide in you and you to abide in God?

As a Christian you have experienced personally that God the Father has sent Jesus Christ to be the Savior—your own Savior, as well as the Savior of the world. Now, in what ways can you live out the truths of 1 John 4:13-15 in today's tasks? What differences will there be in your attitudes? in your actions? *End today's Quiet Time by writing at least one specific way you will try to put the truths of 1 John 4:13-15 to work in your life today.*

WEEK 1: THE INDWELLING CHRIST
DAY 2: USING YOUR BIBLE AS A SOURCE OF
CHRISTIAN GROWTH

Read Psalms 119:11; 40:8. Memorize Psalm 119:11.

Each day you will be given a few Bible verses to study. Your daily Quiet Time should always focus on Scripture. The indwelling Christ will speak to your heart as you read the Word of God.

Do you have a good study Bible? All Bibles in the English language are translations. One popular Bible used by many youth is *The Living Bible*. It is a paraphrase, not a translation. The original books of the Bible were written in ancient Hebrew and Greek. Because the King James Version was first published in the early 1600s, its wording is often hard for readers in the twentieth century. Try to find at least one of these Bible translations:

New American Standard Bible (NASB)
New International Version of the Bible (NIV)
New Living Translation (NLT)

If you did not grow up attending Sunday School, you may have a problem finding books, chapters, and verses in the Bible. Using the index in the front of your Bible, you will soon learn where they are.

All of today's verses are in Psalms; you will find Psalms exactly in the middle of your Bible. *Find and read Psalm 119:11.* Where did the writer keep the Word of God?

IN _____

One way we say "I memorized it" is "I learned it by heart." The writer of Psalm 119:11 used that same word *heart* in saying where he kept God's Word. The last part of that verse tells one great value of memorizing Scripture. What is that value?

_____

Memorizing God's Word can help you keep from sinning against God. *Now turn to and read Psalm 40:8.* If you don't have a Bible in your **hand,** where can you keep a supply of Scripture for use in any emergency?

_____

No other advice in this book will have greater value for your growth as a Christian than this one: MEMORIZE SCRIPTURE ON A REGULAR SCHEDULE! To help you get started, 11 verses are printed on the middle pages of your book. Cut them into pocket-sized cards. The first verse to learn is Psalm 119:11. Memorize one verse each week.

Why bother to learn the exact words of a Scripture verse? Because it's actually easier to recall a verse word for word. It's easier to meditate on a verse when you can repeat it again and again in your mind. Memorized verses give you assurance as a Christian—in fighting temptations to sin, in telling others about Christ, in explaining what you believe. And God wants you to know His Holy Word.

BEGIN NOW! Carry the verses with you. Start learning one verse on Monday of each week. Write the verses and display them in prominent places—on the bathroom mirror, on your desk, near the telephone. You will find that, by disciplining your mind, you can use the bits of time you now waste each day. You can be memorizing while riding, walking, waiting, or resting.

Reviewing daily all verses learned will reinforce them in your memory.

LEARN YOUR VERSES AS THOUGH YOUR SPIRITUAL GROWTH DEPENDED ON IT . . . BECAUSE IT DOES!

WEEK 1: THE INDWELLING CHRIST
DAY 3: LEARNING TO PRAY

Read Matthew 6:9-13.
Quote from memory Psalm 119:11

Do you like to talk with your closest friends? Of course! You will also like to talk with your Lord. You don't need to say words like "Thee" and "Thou dost." God knows the words you normally use. He wants you to speak to Him as a child would speak to a father. Share with Him your attitudes, your fears, your desires, and your frustrations. He will understand. He will respond to your prayers.

Jesus' first followers asked Him to teach them to pray. In response He gave them a Model Prayer, which is often called the Lord's Prayer. You can find this Model Prayer in Matthew 6:9-13. *Look up Matthew in the index to your Bible. Or try opening your Bible one fourth of the way from the back.* Either way, you'll find Matthew at the beginning of the New Testament, the second big section of your Bible.

Read carefully Matthew 6:9-13. Note the kinds of things Jesus included in His Model Prayer. *Copy the Model Prayer on the blank lines on the next page. Begin with "Our Father." Match each phrase or sentence to one part of the out-*

TOPICS IN THE MODEL PRAYER	THE MODEL PRAYER
ADDRESSING GOD PROPERLY (v. 9)	_____ _____
SHOWING RESPECT FOR GOD'S NAME (v. 9)	_____ _____
COMMITTING OURSELVES AND ALL ON EARTH TO GOD'S PLANS (v. 10)	_____ _____ _____
ASKING GOD TO PROVIDE FOR OUR NEEDS (NOT OUR WANTS) (v. 11)	_____ _____
ASKING GOD FOR FORGIVENESS (v. 12)	_____ _____
ASKING GOD FOR PROTECTION (v. 13)	_____ _____
DECLARING GOD'S RULE OVER US TO BE OUR GREATEST WISH (v. 13)	_____ _____
ENDING OUR PRAYER PROPERLY (v. 13, KJV)	_____ _____

line on the left.
Now use the outline of Jesus' Model Prayer and express your own prayer.

Read 2 Corinthians 5:17; Colossians 1:27.

As you develop your Quiet Time day by day, you are aware that some basic changes are happening in your life. *Find and read 2 Corinthians 5:17.*

As you read 2 Corinthians 5:17, you will realize what has happened in your life. Three key words sum things up. *Write them in the proper places below.*

Your _____ life is passing away.

Your _____ life is coming into being.

All of these changes are made by _____.
Yes, Christ makes the difference between your old and your new life. You are being changed. You are being made different from other people who do not know Jesus Christ. You are being made different from what you yourself were before you gave your life to Him.

Now look at Colossians 1:27. The last part of that verse tells who is changing your life from old to new. According to Colossians 1:27, where is Christ right now?_____

_____

_____

_____

Do those two simple little words "in you" remind you of a diagram you have seen in this SURVIVAL KIT? Do you remember seeing a hand with its fingers? *Complete this phrase on the palm in the diagram.*

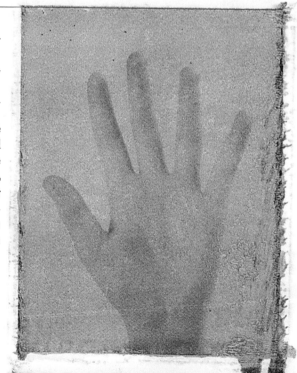

Christ is "in you." He is "the indwelling Christ, controlling all." Because of this, your life is changing day by day.

Habits are hard to break. As the Lord's Holy Spirit within your life takes the fun out of your old habits, **do not let them continue.** In prayer, lay them before God's throne and ask Him to remove them.

List some old habits or actions that have already become flat and tasteless to you.

_____   _____

_____   _____

Never forget that Jesus was willing to die for you! Thank Him for that in your daily Quiet Time. Ask Him to keep on taking away your old habits.

WEEK 1: THE INDWELLING CHRIST
DAY 5: A BASIC PRINCIPLE TO CHOOSE BY

Read 1 Corinthians 10:31. Quote from memory Psalm 119:11.

The Christian faith does not have a long list of do's and don'ts for you to observe. (Beware of those who try to give you one!)

Instead, there is a simple principle to choose by. It is stated most clearly in *1 Corinthians 10:31. Find and read that verse; then state the principle here.*

WHATEVER YOU _ _, _ _ IT _ _ _ FOR THE <u>G</u> _ _ _ _ OF <u>G</u> _ _.

Paul, the writer of 1 Corinthians, made these points very clear:
• Our conduct is a statement of the life we now have in Christ.
• All we do should bring glory to God.

Now apply the basic principle you have just learned. A new Christian was faced with a choice. His best friend, with whom he had smoked marijuana many times, offered him a "drag." He feared that if he refused, his friend would reject him. He desired very much to continue the relationship, hoping he might be able to share Christ with his friend later.

WHAT SHOULD THE NEW CHRISTIAN DO? *Underline your answer.*

A. Take one small puff and then decline to take any more.
B. Scold the friend for smoking marijuana.
C. Avoid the issue by making some sort of excuse.
D. Decline, explaining frankly that he had rather not–that since he has become a Christian, Christ has been taking away his desire to smoke pot.

I hope you underlined the last suggestion. This alone would bring the greatest glory to God, wouldn't it?

You will be faced constantly with choices such as this. You need not act like a self-righteous fanatic. A loving and gentle spirit will help you communicate that you have definite standards for your own conduct although you do not condemn others. People will respect you for that spirit!

You have already learned what a help the Word of God can be in making choices between right and wrong. Your Scripture memory verse should remind you of that fact every time you repeat it. *Write Psalm 119:11 in the margin.*

The verses printed on the middle pages of your SURVIVAL KIT are quoted from the **New American Standard Bible**. Maybe you'd rather memorize them instead from another translation. If so, feel free! Mabe you'd like to write your own Scripture memory cards. Writing the verses word for word, in whatever translation you prefer, is another good way to help you learn them more quickly.

Do you know and feel more of Christ's indwelling presence than you did a week ago?

The following weeks of this SURVIVAL KIT will not tell you day by day to have a Quiet Time. But you have already discovered for yourself how much a daily Quiet Time can mean in your spiritual growth as a new Christian. Each day's material in the SURVIVAL KIT will always include some Scripture verses for you to read and study, five days a week. During your Quiet Time on the sixth and seventh day of each week, use your Sunday School lesson, your Discipleship Training material, or other Bible passages.

Don't forget to **pray** as you meditate on God's Word. A daily time for prayer and Bible study can be one of the best ways the indwelling Christ makes His presence felt as He controls your life!

Read Romans 12:4-5 and memorize the verses.

There should be no "Lone Ranger" Christians in God's family! The very act of becoming a follower of Jesus Christ is an act of commitment to others who have already vowed to follow Him forever.

Can you imagine a family without a baby being born into it? That's possible. But can you imagine a baby surviving without someone to love it and to care for it? Hardly!

Babies do not **survive** if left alone. They need constant love, care, and attention. To survive, they must be surrounded by a family—people who are concerned about their survival. Apart from the family of God, you will not grow much spiritually. That family is called by several names: the **church,** the **called-out ones,** the **body of Christ,** the **living stones.** (You will learn more about these names later.)

Open your Bible to Romans 12:4-5. These verses state one central truth about the family of God, the church. That truth can be formulated almost like an equation. *Fill in the missing letters, based on what you read in Romans 12:4-5.*

M _ _ _   M _ _ _ _ _ _   (OR PARTS) = 1 _ _ _ _

A central truth about the church is its oneness. The Scriptures say, "We are **one** body in Christ." So you should have written the equation like this:

MANY MEMBERS (OR PARTS) = 1 BODY

Romans 12:4-5 is the verse you are to memorize this week. Here it is, quoted from the **New American Standard Bible.** *See whether you can already complete it by filling in four key words, each of which is used twice in the verse.*

"Just as we have _____ _____ in _____

_____ and all the _____ do not have the same function,

so we, who are _____, are _____

_____ in Christ" (Romans 12:4-5, NASB).

You should have completed Romans 12:4-5, **New American Standard Bible,** like this: "Just as we have many members in one body and all the members do not have the same function, so we, who are many, are one body in Christ." If you are going to have a natural, healthy growth, it is necessary for you to be in the fellowship of a church. You will find among church members the love, nurture, and care that permit **growth** to take place.

If you have not yet professed Christ publicly and been baptized into the membership of a church, you should do so at **once.** Don't ever think church membership is an option or something to be delayed. IT IS THE FIRST STEP TO SURVIVAL AS A GROWING CHRISTIAN.

WEEK 2: ONE BODY—ITS LIFE
DAY 2: THE CHURCH, A BODY

Read 2 Timothy 1:8-10; Ephesians 4:1-4.

Do you know the meaning of the word *church*? It is a translation of a Greek word in one of the original languages of the Bible: **ekklesia,** meaning **"called-out ones."**

Visualize a large group of people who live by their own personal whims. Christ approaches them and calls out: "Follow Me! Separate yourselves from others who live by their personal desires. Be My disciples!"

Some hear Him . . . and then turn away. Others make a clear decision: They walk away from the large group. They come to Christ. They have decided to follow Him.

These are the "called-out ones." They are the church.

You will see the words "called" and "calling" in the Bible passages listed for your reading today. Look first at 2 Timothy 1:8-10. Find in those verses the answers to these questions.

Who calls us out? _____

In whom are we called out? _____

God calls us out "in Christ Jesus."

The character of the "called-out ones" is described in Ephesians 4:1-4. *Find and read those verses now.* The power Christ gives us lets us live a new lifestyle. List here some of the characteristics of this new lifestyle made possible by Christ for the "called-out ones."

_____   _____

_____   _____

_____   _____

The lifestyle pictured in Ephesians 4:1-4 is clear. Humility, gentleness, patience, forbearance, love—these characteristics will show in the lives of Christ's "called-out ones."

Which characteristic would you most desire for others to see in your life today? *Mark your initials beside it in the list above.*

Here is a deep thought: Christ will not **give** you that characteristic. You see, He **is** that characteristic. Christ is humble, gentle, patient, loving, and all the rest. You need only to let Christ be Lord, and He will reveal to those you meet this day that lovely part of His nature which now lives in you!

Did you notice a familiar two-word phrase in Ephesians 4:4? Note that the "called-out ones" are referred to in that verse as **"one body."** Tomorrow you will continue thinking about this important idea.

WEEK 2: ONE BODY—ITS LIFE
DAY 3: NO DIVISIONS IN THE BODY

Read 1 Corinthians 12:14-27. Quote from memory Romans 12:4-5.

Perhaps you have already discovered that Jesus, during His ministry on this earth, often taught His followers by means of storytelling. Books of the Bible written by the apostle Paul contain few stories. Your Bible reading for today sounds like one of the parables told by Jesus. But in this case, Paul was doing the storytelling.

In 1 Corinthians 12:14-27 Paul compared Christ's "called-out ones" to parts of a human body. Each part is unique but connected to the rest. The indwelling

Christ is equally present in the hand, in the foot, or in an inner organ. All are interdependent; no member can **survive** without help from other members.

What a powerful description Paul gave of life in the body of Christ!

Your growth in the Christian life is related directly to those you are related to in the body of Christ. When one suffers, all hurt. When one rejoices, all are happy.

That's why baptism and the Lord's Supper are celebrated when all the members who make up the church are **together.** For example, all the members celebrate when you, by your baptism, give witness to a new life in Christ that already has begun. In the Lord's Supper, all the members share symbolically with you the life provided by the death of Christ. These are events in the life of the body of Christ. They cannot be enjoyed by those who are not a part of the body.

How much do you know about baptism and the Lord's Supper? Stop now and test your knowledge.

BAPTISM AND THE LORD'S SUPPER

Mark **B** for **baptism** or **LS** for **Lord's Supper** beside each of the following below:

_____ 1. Described in 1 Corinthians 11:23-26.

_____ 2. Described in Romans 6:4.

_____ 3. Experienced personally by a Christian one time only.

_____ 4. Experienced personally by a Christian many times.

_____ 5. Symbolizes Jesus' broken body and shed blood.

_____ 6. Symbolizes Jesus' death and resurrection.

_____ 7. Symbolizes a Christian's death to sin and new life in Christ.

_____ 8. Commanded to be done by all who follow Christ.

_____ 9. Usually described as one of the two ordinances of the church.

Answers: 1—LS; 2—B; 3—B; 4—LS; 5—LS; 6—B; 7—B; 8—either or both; 9—either.

Read 1 Peter 2:1-10; Ephesians 2:19-22.

You are learning two Bible verses that speak of that "ONE BODY," made up of all who follow Christ. Fill in the key words "one," "body" and "members" at the proper places in the verses.

"As we have many _____ in _____ _____, and all

_____ have not the same office: So we, being many, are

_____ _____ in Christ" (Romans 12:4-5, KJV).

Read two passages of Scripture that use a different figure of speech to picture the church: 1 Peter 2:1-10 and Ephesians 2:19-22.

In these passages, the "called-out ones" are described as a **building** rather than as a body. Christ is "the head of the body, the church" (Colossians 1:18). But He is also the "chief corner stone" of the **building** (1 Peter 2:6). We are described as "living stones." We are being constructed into a "spiritual house," a "holy temple."

When stonemasons erect a wall from stones, they must chip away on each one, smoothing and shaping it. Soon it has the proper form to be fitted against the stones around it. This shows why you must be a part of a church to grow properly. GOD'S SHAPING PROCESS IN YOUR LIFE REQUIRES YOU TO BE RELATED PROPERLY TO OTHER "LIVING STONES." He chips away at your character until you are "bonded together" with the other "living stones."

Some stones have rough edges. *Reread 1 Peter 2:1.* According to that verse, what are some of the "rough edges" our Lord may be expected to chip away from our lives as we come to Him?

Actually, two kinds of "stones" are mentioned in 1 Peter 2:1-10. You and I and all other Christians are like stones with rough edges— envy, hypocrisy, and all the other evils listed in verse 1. But Jesus Christ, our sinless Lord and Savior, is the "choice" or "precious" or "valuable" cornerstone described in verse 6.

Now look again at Ephesians 2:19-22. What "cement" bonds together the "living stones" that make up the church?_____

Christ Jesus Himself joins us with one another in His church. According to verse 22, what is the sole purpose for the existence of this building made up of believers?

_____

Isn't it great to know that you and your fellow believers help to form a building in which God's Holy Spirit lives? Are you beginning to realize that you, as an individual member of the **body** (or the **"building"**) of believers, truly need the others who are "called-out ones"? *List here two areas in your life as a Christian which you know will not develop properly apart from your fellowship with other Christians.*

_____

_____

Whatever you just wrote, be sure to pray about it when you have your daily Quiet Time. Ask God to help you grow in relationship with your fellow believers.

Also, don't forget to review the verses you have been memorizing thus far! Place a check mark beside the reference of each verse that you can repeat aloud, right now.

           Psalm 119:11 _____   Romans 12:4-5 _____

WEEK 2: ONE BODY—ITS LIFE
DAY 5: NEW LIFE IN THE BODY!

Read Acts 2:42-47; 4:32-35. Quote from memory Psalm 119:11 and Romans 12:4-5.

These passages boggle the minds of twentieth-century Christians until they discover for themselves the true meaning of the church. Christians, from time to time, sold a portion of their assets and shared it through the apostles as others in the body (church) had needs.

Those who had more than they needed shared with other people. As they did, they were confident that God would, in turn, supply all their needs.

They shared far more than wealth. They shared their very lives with one another—eating, praying, sharing in Bible study, and teaching. Their lifestyle showed that they had been "called out" from other people. The life of the "called-out ones" was not marked by the closed, selfish spirit found among unbelievers. Instead, they had a special family life together.

The fellowship you share with other believers is a vital part of your growth in Christ. Plunge deeply into the family of God and develop relationships with those who are your new brothers and sisters in the family.

Now make a brief comparative study of Acts 2:42-45 and Acts 4:32-35. Both of these passages describe three important aspects of the church—then and now. *Read the verses marked on the first line of the chart. Then try to complete the summary sentence. Do the same thing with the second and third lines.*

ACTS 2	ACTS 4	LIFE IN THE CHURCH
44	32	Church members are _____ _____ in Christ.
45	34-35	Church members should _____ their lives.
42-43	33	Church members should _____ their Lord.

You probably had little difficulty remembering that church members are **one body** in Christ. And a little while ago you read that church members should **share** their lives. What did you write on the third line? **Proclaim? witness for? tell people about?** Any of those would be correct.

Read Acts 2:45 once more. Which would be more difficult for **you**: to **sell** a personal possession to help a needy member of the church body or to be on the **receiving end** of such a gift? Why?

_____

_____

Now write below Romans 12:4-5, (This is one of your memory passages about the church as one body in Christ.)

_____

_____

Read 1 Corinthians 13:1-13. Memorize 1 Peter 4:10.

You have read one of the most beautiful chapters in the Bible. It is also one of the most famous passages in world literature.

What is the greatest thing in the world, according to the verses that you have read today? _____ If you read 1 Corinthians 13 in the King James Version, you may have written the word *charity* on that blank line. Almost all other translations of the Bible use "love."

Love is the greatest thing in the world! God **is** that love, and Christ's love in you flows to others. THE BODY OF CHRIST IS MADE TO REVEAL LOVE! Unbelievers are "called out" to be changed by the love of Christ.

25

Now take a closer look at 1 Corinthians 13 (sometimes called "The Love Chapter"). In verses 1-3, which of these qualities are described as being inferior to love? *(Check the boxes.)*

- ❏ Great spiritual knowledge
- ❏ Powers of speaking
- ❏ Being willing to die for truth
- ❏ Generosity to the poor
- ❏ Mighty faith
- ❏ All of these qualities

Did you realize that **all of these qualities** are mentioned in 1 Corinthians 13:1-3? Maybe you checked that last box; or maybe you just checked each of the other boxes individually. **Remember:** The point made by Paul, the writer of 1 Corinthians, is that **all** of these qualities, good and even great as they are, are not as great as **love.**

Surprise! All of these qualities are yours as a Christian. God is love. And the Son of God, the indwelling Christ, will make these qualities of love more and more apparent in your life as you let Him live in you.

Verse

_____

These pictures match two figures of speech Paul used in 1 Corinthians 13:11-12. *Mark the verse number below the picture it matches:*

Verse

_____

Verse 12 describes our limited human knowledge as being like dim shadows seen in a mirror. Verse 11 compares it to the babbling of a child. That's why knowledge is not as great as **love.**

When God added you to His body, He made you a **working member** of it. He provided you with **spiritual energies,** called **"gifts."** Think of the gifts of the Spirit as "riverbeds" through which Christ's love flows. The faster a river flows, the deeper the riverbed is cut. As God's love flows through you, your gifts deepen. Their **purpose** is to let more of Christ's love flow to others! Your "work" for Him is to be a channel for His love. That is why He has given you gifts.

This truth is made plain in the verse you should be memorizing during the week: 1 Peter 4:10. Write it here.

WEEK 3: ONE BODY–ITS SERVICE
DAY 2: EVERY MEMBER HAS A FUNCTION

Read 1 Corinthians 12:4-7.

EVERY MEMBER OF A BODY OF CHRIST HAS A FUNCTION!

God added you to the body to be a working member of it. When He did so, He gave you spiritual energies called gifts. Two of these gifts are basic to all the other gifts. They are the gift of **service** and the gift of **giving.** You should be using these two gifts today. As you are obedient to Christ, the Head of the body, He will deepen your channel of love—your riverbed. Other gifts will mature in you. Although you now possess all the gifts He ever plans for you to use, many require a deeper level of maturity to be exercised.

There is a difference between **gifts** and **talents.** A **gift** is a spiritual power possessed only by Christians. On the other hand, either Christians or non-Christians can possess talents. For example: Piano playing is a **talent** and can be used for either man or God. Faith is a **gift** and is used to glorify God.

On the top of the next page list some of the talents you possess that you can use to glorify God rather than only to bring admiring looks toward yourself.

Be sure to check your memorization of 1 Peter 4:10. Now look at another part of the Bible that also tells about gifts. Read 1 Corinthians 12:4-6. In whatever translation you are using, it should be clear that each of these three short verses shows within it a contrast. Summarize those three contrasts by completing this simple chart.

1 CORINTHIANS12	DIFFERENT	THE SAME
Verse 4	gifts	Spirit
Verse 5		
Verse 6		

All the words you have written in the "DIFFERENT" column of the chart should have something to do with **gifts** (spiritual energies given to Christians) and how these are used. All the words you have written in "THE SAME" column of the chart should be names for the One who gives you these gifts.

Why does the Lord God through His Spirit give you these gifts? The purpose is stated in 1 Corinthians 12:7. *Read that verse; then place a check mark beside the right answer.*

_____ For the good of the person receiving the gift.

_____ For the good of all, the common good.

You should have checked the second of the two answers.

WEEK 3: ONE BODY—ITS SERVICE
DAY 3: OBEDIENCE

Read Romans 12:1-8. Quote from memory 1 Peter 4:10.

Would you trust a thousand dollars to the care of a servant who did not obey your commands? Of course not!

God has provided you with many spiritual gifts. Before they will become available for your use, however, you must first prove yourself obedient to Christ, the Head of the body.

Look now at the title for "Day 3." The key to the gifts God gives you is **obedience.** God gives gifts to those He can **trust** to obey Him.

Read Romans 12:1-3 to help you realize what obedience requires. Here are five key words or phrases from those verses.

TRANSFORMED   CONFORMED

SACRIFICE

THINK HIGHLY   WILL OF GOD

In Romans 12:1-3, two of these five key words or phrases are used to state what you **must not do** if you are obedient to your Lord. The other three are used to state what you **must do.** *Try now to write those five statements briefly, using the key words and phrases from Romans 12:1-3.*

WHAT YOU MUST NOT DO: _____

_____

WHAT YOU MUST DO: _____

_____

_____

Now check what you have written by this example. (Your statements may vary somewhat, according to which version you are using.)

WHAT YOU MUST NOT DO: Be conformed to this world.
Think too highly of yourself.
WHAT YOU MUST DO: Give yourself as a living sacrifice.
Be transformed (by the indwelling Christ).
Do the will of God.

Now here's another thought question for your meditation during Quiet Time today: Do you struggle with the thought that you are to be **obedient** to Christ? If so, can you list some reasons for your struggle? What parts of your value system for life are being challenged by the call for obedience?

_____

Read 1 Corinthians 1:4-5; 16:15-16.

Your next reading includes a few verses from the first chapter of 1 Corinthians, plus a few verses from the last chapter. *Mark an X beside the reference of the passage that mentions the basic gift of service.*

_____ 1 Corinthians 1:4-8   _____ 1 Corinthians 16:15-16

The gift of **service,** mentioned in 1 Corinthians 16:15-16, is sometimes called the gift of administration. The word literally describes one who **serves** as a **waiter at tables.** It is used to mean any **activity of service** motivated by the love of Christ within us.

Serving the Lord in the simple things is an expression of obedience. Christ was willing to wash the feet of His disciples. It was not "beneath His dignity." That **same** Christ is now Lord of **your life!** If you are not faithful to Him in small things, should you expect Him to give you greater ministries to perform?

Look again at 1 Corinthians 1:4-8. From these verses, do you get the assurance that you have immediate use of some gifts upon receiving Christ as Lord and Savior?

Look again at 1 Corinthians 16:15-16. These verses mention that Stephanas' family is performing a task. What words does your translation use to describe the task?

_____

Actually, 1 Corinthians 16:15 says in the original language that this family of Christians had devoted themselves to using the gift of **service.**

Whom were they serving?

_____

The word *saints* in 1 Corinthians 16:15 means Christians, the "called-out ones," not people who are considered "super Christians" or people whose names are on a special list.

According to 1 Corinthians 16:16, how are we to treat members of the body of Christ who exercise the gift of service?

_____

_____

We are to follow the leadership of those who exercise the gift of service; we are to submit or subject ourselves to them.

You possess the **gift of service!** You may not exercise it by sewing for widows, as Dorcas did, but you have it nonetheless. Christ's presence within your life will express itself first by teaching you the great value of serving others. It is the basic gift for all ministries to follow, for all years to come. You can begin to exercise it **today.**

Pray about the answer to this question: IN WHAT WAY, **TODAY,** DOES CHRIST CALL YOU TO SERVE OTHERS IN THE BODY OF CHRIST?

Now do a little checking. How well are you "surviving" as a new Christian? **Remember:** You have Christ's promise in John 10:28 that you will never lose your relationship to Him as Lord and Savior. But it's still good to check up on yourself now and then.

It has now been nearly three weeks since you began using your *Survival Kit for Youth.* How many days in those three weeks have you had a Quiet Time, including prayer and Bible study? *Circle the number of days.*

1 2 3 4 5 6 7 8 9 10 11 12 13 14 15 16 17 18 19 20

How many Scripture verses have you committed to memory? *Underline references for the ones you can repeat aloud right now.*

Psalm 119:11   Romans 12:4-5   1 Peter 4:10

WEEK 3: ONE BODY–ITS SERVICE
DAY 5: THE GIFT OF GIVING

Read 2 Corinthians 8:1-5; 9:6-15. Quote from memory Psalm 119:11; Romans 12:4-5; and 1 Peter 4:10.

"Giving" is a Bible word describing A PERSON'S DELIBERATELY PART-
ING WITH POSSESSIONS SO THAT A CHANGE OF OWNERSHIP IS
BROUGHT ABOUT. Such giving is the result of the Holy Spirit's work. When
you recognize that Jesus Christ is the **owner** of all you possess, it isn't hard to
share! You will have problems only when you continue to consider possessions
as yours. The key is **letting the Spirit lead you** to give what you have in min-
istering to others. You do this, firmly believing that God will supply your needs
continually and that God is perfectly able to replenish your supply. After all, if
God **causes** you to give, He can be trusted to care for your own future needs.

Read 2 Corinthians 8:1-5. Do you think the Christians described in these verses could really "afford" to give liberally? Why or why not?

_____

_____

Did you write such words as "poor," "poverty," "trouble," "affliction"?
Members of the churches in Macedonia were not rich; yet they gave.

Now read 2 Corinthians 9:6-15. Among verses 6-10, which two verses give
strongest assurance that God will supply the source of your giving? Verse
_____ and verse _____.

Verses 8 and 10 give this assurance. In verse 11, what is the ultimate purpose
for your being enriched?

_____

_____

Your generous giving, made possible by God's generous giving, will result in
"many thanksgivings unto God." According to 2 Corinthians 9:13, how does the
watching world respond to the spectacle of Christians giving to help one another? Who will get the greatest benefit from your use of the gift of giving?

_____

Many people will give glory to God because Christians give to help one another. What specific commitment is Christ calling you to make as you begin to
exercise this basic gift of giving? **(Remember:** He is more interested in
whether your giving is an **act of obedience** than He is in **how much** you
give.)

Read Galatians 5:13-18. Memorize Galatians 5:22-23.

Did you know that you now have **two natures** rather than one?

Since birth, you have had an old nature. Since your **new birth,** you have had a **new nature** also. One seeks to exalt self; the other seeks to cause **the love of God to flow through you.**

Think of the old nature within you as though it were the law of gravity. This law constantly pulls objects downward. It never stops working.

Now see what the Scriptures say about your two natures. *Find and read Galatians 5:13-18.* In verses 13-14 you will note a key word used twice. This word tells how **your new nature** functions in your life as a Christian. What is that key word? _____

One way your new nature functions in **love** is through exercising one of your two basic gifts, the gift of **giving.**

Yes, your new nature functions in **love.** But not your old nature! According to Galatians 5:15, what are some signs that the old nature is in control?

_____

In Galatians 5:15 Paul pictured wild animals biting and hurting one another. It's terrible to see people acting that way—especially Christian people! In verse 17 Paul explained how such a thing can happen. Read that verse from the **Revised Standard Version:** "For the desires of the flesh are against the Spirit, and the desires of the Spirit are against the flesh; for these are opposed to each other, to prevent you from doing what you would" (Galatians 5:17, RSV).

Read aloud the verse quoted, substituting "your old nature" for "the flesh" and "your new nature" for "the Spirit." After hearing the verse read that way, do you realize that **your choice** determines which nature will be in control of your life? Choosing either will "prevent you from doing" what the other nature would cause you to do.

Galatians 5:16 states the **condition** you must meet for the law of the new nature to be in effect in your life. What is that condition?

_____

Tomorrow you will learn more of what it means to **"walk in the Spirit."**

Read Galatians 2:20.

When we speak of a person's **"spirit,"** we are speaking about **the total of what he is**—his thoughts, motives, impulses, desires, and actions. Since your birth, your spirit has expressed itself through your body. Until now, you have been a slave to the **old nature.** That nature has controlled your **spirit** and expressed itself through your body. This expression was sin, self-exaltation.

But notice that the word *Spirit* in Galatians 5:16 has a capital **S.** When you became a Christian, Christ broke the old nature's rule over your life. You now have a **new nature.** The indwelling Christ controls your life through His Holy Spirit. The old nature sought to exalt self; the **new nature** seeks to **cause the love of God to flow through you.**

Don't think of your new nature as **"it."** In Galatians 2:20 you are given the **name** of the One who is your new nature. What is that name?

_____

According to that verse, complete the following sentence:
Since I have died with Christ, He now _____ within me!

Christ lives within you—what an awesome statement! And you "live by faith in the Son of God." You can remember the word *faith* in this way:

> **F** ORSAKING
> **A** LL
> **I**
> **T** RUST
> **H** IM!

33

What do you think Galatians 2:20 means by stating that you are to live by **faith in the Son of God?**

_____

_____

It is through your own choice that your new nature, the indwelling Christ, can control your life. You must surrender yourself completely to Him. You must choose to let Him be your Lord and Master. And in making that decision, **you belong to your choice.** You become Christ's, and not your own.

WEEK 4: TWO NATURES—PART ONE: THE NEW NATURE
DAY 3: UNDER CHRIST'S CONTROL

Read Colossians 3:1-7. Quote from memory Galatians 5:22-23.

Once again, recognize that **Christ lives in you.** He Himself is the new nature you have been given. Often, you may want to ask Christ to **give** you something such as love, power, gentleness, righteousness. He does not **give** you these things; He **is** these things!

Instead of giving you the characteristics you desire, He has given you **the source of those characteristics.** This is your **new nature.**

The characteristics of Christ, your new nature, are expressed beautifully in the passage you should memorize this week, Galatians 5:22-23. Have you already cut out a pocket-sized Scripture memory card with that verse on it? **Remember:** You may use the ready-made cards from the middle pages of this SURVIVAL KIT, or you may prepare your own cards. You may memorize your verses from the **New American Standard Bible** (as printed in your SURVIVAL KIT) or from another translation.

Here are three of Christ's characteristics listed in Galatians 5:22-23, as they are translated in several of the more recent versions. *Try to match each one of them with a different word that has the same meaning, as translated in Galatians 5:22-23, King James Version.*

PATIENCE: _____

FAITHFULNESS: _____

SELF-CONTROL: _____

Did you write **"longsuffering," "faith,"** and **"temperance"**?

In Colossians 3:1-7 the apostle Paul told more about your new nature. *Read those verses. Then turn back to Colossians 2:12-13.* How does Colossians 2:12 throw light on the expression "risen" or "raised to life" which Paul used in Colossians 3:1?

_____

_____

_____

Remember: Your baptism does not **give** you your new nature. You already have Christ living in you. Your baptism is only a picture–a symbol–of what has happened to you. On the lines above, did you write something like this? "My old life has been symbolically buried with Christ, and I have now been resurrected into a new life with Christ."

Three times in five verses Paul called on you to make a personal choice as a Christian—once in Colossians 3:1, again in verse 2, and a third time in verse 5. How does your Bible state these three choices?

VERSE 1: _____

VERSE 2: _____

VERSE 5: _____

Here's how the **Good News Bible** states those three choices: "Set your hearts on the things that are in heaven. Keep your minds fixed on things there, not on things here on earth. You must put to death, then, the earthly desires at work in you" (Colossians 3:1b,2,5a, GNB).

Based on what you have learned from these verses, what commitment would you like to make for your life today?

_____

_____

_____

Read 2 Corinthians 4:6-10.

The following two words have special meanings for you as a Christian; they have something to do with your **new nature.**

CONTROLLER   **CONTAINER**

Second Corinthians 4:6-10 uses different figures of speech to describe your new nature. *Read those verses now.* Which verse explains the new meaning of the word *container* as it applies to you? Verse _____ What word in **verse 7** describes what is inside this container?

36

Because of the **treasure** inside the container—in other words, because of the indwelling Christ within your life—you will experience victory. Second

Corinthians 4:8-9 pictures this victory in a series of four contrasts. How does your Bible phrase those four contrasts in verses 8-9? *Write them here.*

WE ARE BUT

_____

_____

_____

_____

WE ARE NOT

_____

_____

_____

_____

Here's how you should have written those four contrasts if you were using the **New American Standard Bible;** other versions use other words that have the same meanings.

WE ARE	BUT WE ARE NOT
afflicted in every way	crushed
perplexed	despairing
persecuted	forsaken
struck down	destroyed

There's no doubt about it! Becoming a Christian is an act in which you receive a new nature. You can now be **controlled** by the love of Christ. You are a **container** for a new life—**the life of Christ.**

You are to be **controlled** by that life. You no longer live for yourself; instead, you live for Christ. He is to be given freedom to use you, to execute His plans on His planet. Second Corinthians 4:7 compares your life to a clay pot, used in Bible times to preserve a valuable document. The container was important because of what it contained; otherwise, it had little significance. Of course, **you** are more than a clay pot. You are a person. God neither takes away your dignity nor expects you to become a puppet on a string. Rather, the indwelling Christ brings you to completeness.

This week you are learning Galatians 5:22-23, which lists the fruit Christ's indwelling Spirit will produce in your life. *Can you write by memory the ninefold fruit of the Spirit?*

_____   _____

_____   _____

_____   _____

_____   _____

_____

Read Galatians 5:22-25; Romans 8:28. Quote from memory Psalm 119:11; Romans 12:4-5; 1 Peter 4:10; and Galatians 5:22-23.

An apple tree produces **apples.** It cannot produce **oranges,** because by nature it is an apple tree!

38

Your **new nature** also produces fruit. That fruit is listed in a verse you should know by now. *Write it on the lines on the next page.*

_____

_____

_____

_____

Check your memory of Galatians 5:22-23. Notice that the fruit of the Spirit is not what you **do,** but what you **are.** In each case the fruit describes **character,** not **activity!**

Which of the ninefold fruit of the Spirit is it **impossible** for you to counterfeit in your own strength? The lack of which one in your life troubles you most as a new Christian? *Underline it in the verse above.*

Do you believe Christ can become **all** of these things in you? Of course He can! New Christians often wonder how they can **know** that they have really become Christians. Well, the answer to that question is based, first of all, on a **fact:** You have trusted your life to a trustworthy God. He promised that if you asked Him to forgive you of all your sins, He would do it. YOU ASKED, AND HE DID IT.

Romans 8:28 states the **result** of your new nature taking control of your life. *Be sure to read that verse in a contemporary translation.* The word *God* should appear twice in verse 28. *After you have read Romans 8:28 in a contemporary version, mark which of these statements is more nearly correct.*

❑ Everything turns out for good for people who love God.
❑ God works everything out for good for people who love God.

You marked the second statement, didn't you? God doesn't just "let things happen"; He takes active control of your life, as you yield yourself to Him through the indwelling Christ.

There is a simple decision you make as a Christian—hour by hour, day by day. It is to crown Jesus Christ as Lord of your life. When you do, His nature is in control of you. His nature produces the fruit of the Spirit. You do not have to struggle to be "like Jesus." You simply **let Him be Himself within you: THE INDWELLING CHRIST, CONTROLLING ALL.** WHAT A LIFE!

Read Romans 6:12-18. Memorize Colossians 3:8-10.

"That's just human nature." How many times have you heard people say those words to excuse some undesirable word or deed?

You know that this excuse doesn't work for you any longer. Christ doesn't let Christians get by with living according to human nature. He Himself is your new nature, changing your attitudes and your actions.

Yet your human nature is not dead. It's still there, as it was before you gave your life to Christ. *Read what Romans 6:12-18 has to say about your old nature.*

This passage pictures **sin** as a sort of king, who has the power to rule over you. According to verse 12, the choice is yours: If you "let sin reign" (Romans 6:12, NASB), you must take the consequences.

Your old nature is your human nature. It is the nature of **sin** within you. It was not destroyed when you became a Christian. Rather, it was for the first time **dethroned.** For the first time, sin has no power to control your life . . . except when you **choose** to become a slave to it again. YOU BELONG TO YOUR CHOICE.

Check to see whether you understand:

Who is the new nature within you? _____

Who is the old nature within you? _____

Who decides who will reign over you? _____

Your first answer, of course, should have been **"Christ."** Your second answer might have been worded like any of these:

Myself   **My human nature**   **Sin**   **My sinful self**

And who decides which will reign over you?

You do!

40

Notice the wording of Romans 6:12-13 in the **Good News Bible:** "Sin must no longer rule in your mortal bodies, so that you obey the desires of your natural self. Nor must you surrender any part of yourselves to sin to be used for wicked purposes. Instead, give yourselves to God, as those who have been brought from death to life, and surrender your whole being to him to be used for righteous purposes" (Romans 6:12-13, GNB).

Do you remember a verse that tells one of the best ways to keep from surrendering to sin in your life? It was the first Scripture memory verse you were assigned in this SURVIVAL KIT. *Write it here.*

_____

_____

Be sure to check your accuracy in quoting Psalm 119:11. Then look again at Romans 6:14-18. Remember that sin is dethroned but not dead.

You may choose to **obey** the sinful self, your old nature. Or, you may choose to **obey** Christ, your new nature. And you become the slave of whichever nature you are **obedient** to.

Read Romans 7:15,18-21.

One of the hardest things for a new Christian to realize is this: YOUR OLD NATURE CANNOT BE REFORMED! When you try to live in the old nature and produce the fruit of the new nature, you are frustrated.

Romans 7:15,18-21 pictures a Christian who attempts to do this. Read those verses and summarize in your own words the struggle described.

_____

_____

Did you write something like this?

> **"I want to do good . . . but I can't do it!**
>
> **I don't want to do evil . . . but I do it!"**

Here's a thought question for your daily Quiet Time: In what ways do you identify your own life with the struggle you have just summarized?

_____

_____

Whatever you answer to the thought question, you should find it easy to answer this: Does it seem logical to you that Christ has brought you His indwelling life to live in such a struggle as Romans 7:15,18-21 describes?

Yes _____ No _____

No, it doesn't seem logical. Yet it happens because your old nature cannot be reformed. When you have apple **roots,** you produce apple **fruit.** When you have orange **roots,** you produce orange **fruit.** The nature of the root always determines the nature of the fruit. Your old nature is still producing the same kind of fruit **since** you became a Christian as it did **before** you became a Christian.

The nature of the root always determines the nature of the fruit - Just as the bulb of the tulip produces the tulip flower.

Many a Christian has a tendency to "trust" his old nature too far. He assumes that giving his life to Christ has taken away automatically everything that might ever lead him astray. He forgets that his old nature can never be reformed.

WEEK 5: TWO NATURES—PART TWO: THE OLD NATURE
DAY 3: CIVIL WAR WITHIN

Read Romans 7:22-25; 8:5-6. Quote from memory Colossians 3:8-10.

Would you believe that a **civil war** can go on in your life as a Christian? Such a war takes place when your new nature and your old nature struggle against each other.

Read Romans 7:22-25. The struggle described in those verses is caused by a

Christian who has **not** made a choice. He has not made a clear-cut decision to let the indwelling Christ be the Lord of his life.

Romans 7:23 mentions a frequent result of war: captivity. And Romans 7:24 pictures a hideous situation. Ancient conquerors developed a terrible way of torturing a prisoner: They would bind a corpse to him so tightly that the living man, if he tried to escape, would have to carry the dead man on his back!

In verse 24 the apostle Paul asked a question which shows he may have been thinking about this horrible torture. What is that question?

_____

"Who shall deliver me?" Paul pleaded. "Who will set me free?" Romans 7:25 gives both the **name** and the **title** of the One who can release you from this civil war within. *Write them both here.*

Name: _____   _____

Title: _____

What significance does this title have in bringing to an end the civil war between your two natures?

_____

_____

If **"Jesus Christ"** is truly **"your Lord,"** then He must control your life. You must own His lordship and refuse to obey your old human nature.

The **King James Version** sometimes uses "the old man" and "the new man" where newer translations use "the old nature" and "the new nature," or "the old self" and "the new self." *Look now at Colossians 3:8-10, your memory assignment for this week.* Notice that the portion to be memorized ends with the first part of verse 10, after "the new man" or "the new self" or "the new nature," depending on which Bible translation you prefer to use. *Don't delay beginning to work hard on this passage.*

Read Romans 8:5-6. These two verses contrast two types of life which you may experience as a Christian. One is the life of a Christian who has yielded to the rule of the **old nature.** The other is the life of a Christian who has yielded to the rule of the **new nature.** *Complete this simple chart to show the contrast:*

![logo]	THE OLD NATURE	THE NEW NATURE
Mind-set (v. 5)		
Results (v. 6)		

If you used either the **King James Version** or the **New American Standard Bible,** you should have completed the chart like this:

![logo]	THE OLD NATURE	THE NEW NATURE
Mind-set (v. 5)	the things of the flesh	things of the Spirit
Results (v. 6)	death	life and peace

WEEK 5: TWO NATURES–PART TWO: THE OLD NATURE
DAY 4: VICTORY THROUGH SURRENDER

Read Ephesians 4:22-24; Matthew 5:21-22,27-28; Philippians 4:7-8; Romans 8:37-39.

Today's suggested Bible readings may look long. Actually, the total number of verses is not great. They only happen to come from several different books of the New Testament.

Begin by reading Ephesians 4:22-24. These verses should remind you immediately of Colossians 3:8-10, which you began memorizing Monday. *Try now to write those verses on these lines.*

_____

_____

In both Colossians 3:8 and Ephesians 4:22, the apostle Paul referred to a deliberate decision made by a Christian: to **lay aside,** or **put off,** the old nature. The picture is of a person who has been wearing a suit of clothes for a long, long time. As an **intentional act,** the person takes off his old clothes. They are being discarded—laid aside. They are no longer valuable to the owner. They are not going to be worn again. Such a decision on your part as a new Christian settles the **civil war** within! The old nature is still present, still alive. Its power is rendered helpless, however, by your decision to **lay it aside.** Your choice of a permanent commitment to Jesus Christ allows the full power of His life to be activated within you.

Colossians 3:8-10 lists many characteristics of the old nature. Which ones do you have the greatest desire to lay aside?

_____

In Ephesians 4:23, the apostle Paul referred to the **renewal** of your

_____ .

Read Romans 8:37. Find out what Christ will give you when you make Him Lord and Master of your life. What kind of victory do you experience, or what kind of conqueror do you become?

_____

Did you write **"complete victory"**? **"overwhelmingly conquer"**? **"more than conqueror"**? Romans 8:38-39 continues the same thought, stating that nothing in the entire created order of things can separate you from the love of God through Jesus Christ your Lord.

WEEK 5: TWO NATURES—PART TWO: THE OLD NATURE
DAY 5: ONE DECISION

Read Romans 6:1-11. Quote from memory Psalm 119:11; Romans 12:4-5; 1 Peter 4:10; Galatians 5:22-23; and Colossians 3:8-10.

The apostle Paul didn't like excuses. *Read Romans 6:1-2 to find out whether Paul allowed any excuse for your living as a Christian with your old nature still in control. What unanswerable question did Paul ask in verse 2?*

_____

In Romans 6:3-5, Paul spoke of **baptism** as your public confession that something **already** has taken place in your life. What is that confession?

_____

_____

_____

In baptism you confess that your old sinful self is dead and that you now have been raised to new life in Christ. According to Romans 6:6-7, what has happened to you to free you from the power of the old nature?

_____

Paul said your old nature was **crucified with Christ.** How, then, did Paul explain your life as a Christian, in Romans 6:8-11?

_____

Here's one way to paraphrase what Paul said in Romans 6:8-11: "As far as sin is concerned, you're dead. As far as God is concerned, you're only alive in Jesus Christ." Does that paraphrase make sense to you?

Consider where you are as a new Christian. Have you sometimes boasted to non-Christian friends about your new life in Christ? Then . . . did temper, frustration, resentment, or lust appear in your life? Because of these inner conflicts, did you begin to feel that you were not **really** a Christian after all? Perhaps you felt embarrassed. You tried to "act out" a life of victory before those who watched you. And you knew all the time it was not a **real life** you were living!

The Christian life does not consist of trying to be **like Jesus.** That is an impossibility. Rather, you let Jesus Christ, the Son of God, become the **reigning King** in your life. You give Him the right to guide your thoughts, to control your hands. You settle once and for all the fact that He came into your life to be your **Lord: the One to whom you belong.**

Read Philippians 1:3-11. Memorize Philippians 1:6.

Perhaps when you took Christ as your Lord and Savior, you thought that simple prayer of surrender would give you **all** Christ had to offer you. Well, **you were right!**

In that moment you became a forgiven, freed, Christ-indwelled child of God. In that same moment, however, you also received from God some **rights**. And you were given an **inheritance.** Those rights are yours to claim in the **present.** That inheritance is yours to claim in the **future.**

Salvation, therefore, comes to you in three stages: **past, present,** and **future.** The apostle Paul knew this and explained it to his friends, the Philippian Christians. *Read what Paul wrote in Philippians 1:3-11.*

What did Paul do every time he remembered his Christian friends in Philippi? *(Note v. 3.)* _____

When Paul **thanked God** for the Philippian Christians, what emotion did he always feel when he prayed? *(Note v. 4.)*

_____

As Paul prayed with **joy,** what did he especially thank God for, in relation to those Christian friends in Philippi? *(Note v. 5.)*

_____

Because the Philippians had been Paul's **partners** (or **fellow workers) in spreading the gospel,** where did he say he held them? *(Note v. 7.)*

_____

Paul's feelings of love and affection **in his heart** were so strong that he compared his emotions to the love and affection of whom? *(Note v. 8.)*

_____

SCRIPTURE MEMORY CARDS

See Week 1, Day 2, for instructions
for using your Scripture Memory Cards

(All memory verses are from the *New American Standard Bible.*)

Week 5

TWO NATURES—PART TWO: THE OLD NATURE

Put them all aside: anger, wrath, malice, slander, and abusive speech from your mouth. Do not lie to one another, since you laid aside the old self with its evil practices, and have put on the new self.

Colossians 3:8-10

Week 6

THREE ASPECTS OF SALVATION—PART ONE: ITS BEGINNING AND COMPLETION

For I am confident of this very thing, that He who began a good work in you will perfect it until the day of Christ Jesus.

Philippians 1:6

Week 3

ONE BODY—ITS SERVICE

As each one has received a special gift, employ it in serving one another, as good stewards of the manifold grace of God.

1 Peter 4:10

Week 4

TWO NATURES—PART ONE: THE NEW NATURE

The fruit of the Spirit is love, joy, peace, patience, kindness, goodness, faithfulness, gentleness, self-control; against such things there is no law.

Galatians 5:22-23

Week 1

THE INDWELLING CHRIST

Thy word I have treasured in my heart, that I may not sin against Thee.

Psalm 119:11

Week 2

ONE BODY—ITS LIFE

Just as we have many members in one body and all the members do not have the same function, so we, who are many, are one body in Christ, and individually members one of another.

Romans 12:4-5

Week 6

THREE ASPECTS OF SALVATION—PART ONE: ITS BEGINNING AND COMPLETION

Philippians 1:6

Week 5

TWO NATURES—PART TWO: THE OLD NATURE

Colossians 3:8-10

Week 4

TWO NATURES—PART ONE: THE NEW NATURE

Galatians 5:22-23

Week 3

ONE BODY—ITS SERVICE

1 Peter 4:10

Week 2

ONE BODY—ITS LIFE

Romans 12:4-5

Week 1

THE INDWELLING CHRIST

Psalm 119:11

Week 11

THE FIVE-AND-FIVE PRINCIPLE— FIVE YOU CAN WIN BY WITNESSING

All authority has been given to Me in heaven and on earth. Go therefore and make disciples of all the nations, baptizing them in the name of the Father and the Son and the Holy Spirit, teaching them to observe all that I commanded you; and lo, I am with you always, even to the end of the age.

Matthew 28:18-20

Week 9

FOUR SOURCES OF AUTHORITY—PART TWO: ONE TRUE SOURCE

All Scripture is inspired by God and profitable for teaching, for reproof, for correction, for training in righteousness.

2 Timothy 3:16

Week 10

THE FIVE-AND-FIVE PRINCIPLE—FIVE YOU CAN WIN BY PRAYER

Be anxious for nothing, but in everything by prayer and supplication with thanksgiving let your requests be made known to God.

Philippians 4:6

Week 7

THREE ASPECTS OF SALVATION—PART TWO: A DAILY PROCESS

If while we were enemies, we were reconciled to God through the death of His Son, much more, having been reconciled, we shall be saved by His life.

Romans 5:10

Week 8

FOUR SOURCES OF AUTHORITY—PART ONE: THREE INADEQUATE SOURCES

A natural man does not accept the things of the Spirit of God; for they are foolishness to him, and he cannot understand them, because they are spiritually appraised.

1 Corinthians 2:14

Week 11

THE FIVE-AND-FIVE PRINCI-PLE—FIVE YOU CAN WIN BY WITNESSING

Matthew 28:18-20

Week 10

THE FIVE-AND-FIVE PRINCI-PLE—FIVE YOU CAN WIN BY PRAYER

Philippians 4:6

Week 9

FOUR SOURCES OF AUTHORI-TY—PART TWO: ONE TRUE SOURCE

2 Timothy 3:16

Week 8

FOUR SOURCES OF AUTHORI-TY–PART ONE: THREE INADE-QUATE SOURCES

1 Corinthians 2:14

Week 7

THREE ASPECTS OF SALVA-TION—PART TWO: A DAILY PROCESS

Romans 5:10

Because Paul felt an affection for the Philippian Christians like the love of **Christ Jesus** Himself, he wanted to make sure they understood about the **three aspects of salvation.** No other verse in the Scriptures summarizes this more completely than Philippians 1:6. Note the time frames Paul used in the verse (quoted here from the **Good News Bible**):

PAST   **PRESENT**

"I am sure that God, who **began** this good work in you, **will carry it on** until

FUTURE

it is **finished on the Day of Christ Jesus"** (Philippians 1:6, GNB).

What have you already discovered that your salvation is providing for you in your daily life? *Reread Philippians 1:9-11 to stimulate your thinking; then prayerfully write your answer during your Quiet Time.*

_____

_____

_____

_____

_____

Be still and know that I am God . . . (Psalm 46:10, NIV)

Read Ephesians 2:3-6,8-9,12-13,17-19.

All the Scripture verses in today's study relate to **salvation past:** to that moment when you prayed, asking Christ to enter your life as Lord and Savior. *Read Ephesians 2:3-6.* What did God do at that moment when you trusted Jesus Christ? Verse 5 states it two ways. *Write both of them here.*

1. _____

2. _____

Did you write that God **made you alive together with Christ** and that He **saved you by His grace?** Verse 6 gives two more descriptions of what God did in that moment. *Write them both here.*

3. _____

4. _____

God **raised you up with Christ** and **with Christ made you sit in heavenly places.**

According to verses 8-9, what did you **do** to **deserve** God's forgiveness through Christ? _____

I hope you understood Ephesians 2:8-9 so clearly that you wrote **"Nothing!"** on that blank line. *Read now Ephesians 2:12-13.* What does it mean by "you who were once **far off** have been brought **near** in the blood of Christ" (Ephesians 2:13, RSV)?

Ephesians 2:17-18 makes the matter clear. To whom were you given **instant** and **constant** access at the moment you gave your life to Christ?

_____

As long as you live, you will never stop being amazed at what Christ did for you in that single moment when you prayed and asked Him to enter your life! He called you out of a world in which **self** rules over all your decisions and pleasures. He instantly forgave all the sin and wrong deeds you had ever done. He cleansed you and made you as though you had never sinned. He placed **His own life** inside yours and began to claim your existence as another part of His kingdom. In **a moment of time,** you were forever set free from the worry that at the end of life you would face the judgment of God, be found guilty, and be separated from Him.

Those things are forever settled. Nothing can take away your new life in Christ. You are His . . . **forever!**

WEEK 6: THREE ASPECTS OF SALVATION—PART ONE: ITS BEGINNING AND COMPLETION
DAY 3: BAPTISM OF THE SPIRIT

Read Romans 8:9-11; 1 John 4:12-16. Quote from memory Philippians 1:6.

Salvation past . . . a "point-in-time" event in your salvation! You prayed, confessing the sin of a lifelong, self-controlled existence. You asked Jesus Christ to forgive you of all the sin piled up in your yesterdays. You invited Him to become your Lord.

Today's Scripture passages teach that at that point in time a significant event took place. *Read Romans 8:9-11. Notice how the titles of the Trinity—God, Christ, and the Holy Spirit—are interchanged swiftly in these verses. How many of these titles of the Trinity can you find and list?*

_____	_____
_____	_____
_____	_____
_____	_____

Notice that all these titles for the Trinity are used **almost interchangeably.** Romans 8:9 refers to all three persons of the Trinity; so does verse 11. (Is it hard for you to find a reference to **God the Father** in Romans 8:11? To whom else do you think the following words refer? "He that raised up Christ from the dead.")

Now review these verses again and note the constant use of the phrase "dwells in you" or "lives in you." When you gave your life to Christ, you received the fullness of the Trinity.

The point is this: The Trinity cannot be divided. When you received Christ, you received the Holy Spirit of God. At that moment He came to **dwell** in you, to **live within your life.**

Can you repeat Philippians 1:6 aloud—right now? (Be sure to check your memory by your Bible or by your Scripture Memory Card.)

Now read carefully 1 John 4:12-16. How many persons of the Trinity are mentioned in these verses? *Circle the correct number.*

1   2   3

Of the **three** persons of the Trinity who are mentioned, how many of them are said in these verses to **dwell,** or **live,** in us or to have been **given** or sent to us? *Circle the correct number.*

1   2   3

Did you find **all three?** The **Son** has been **sent**—as your Savior and as the Savior of the world. The **Spirit** has been **given** to you. And **God** Himself **dwells** in you. Isn't this a wonderful truth? You are a **container** for the abiding, indwelling **Son, Spirit,** and **Father.** You need never again pray to receive either Christ or His Holy Spirit or the Heavenly Father. The Triune God is **already** living within your life!

That is a finished act. It will never need to be repeated because Hebrews 13:5 assures you that He will never leave you or forsake you.

WEEK 6: THREE ASPECTS OF SALVATION—PART ONE: ITS BEGINNING AND COMPLETION
DAY 4: SALVATION FUTURE

Read Ephesians 1:13-14; 1 Peter 1:3-9,13

Salvation future . . . the final event in your salvation.

Ephesians 1:13 teaches that you received the Holy Spirit at the moment you gave your life to Christ. *Read that verse now and continue reading it with*

Ephesians 1:14. Do you see the important truth that verse 14 adds? The Holy Spirit, whom you received at the moment of **salvation past,** is just the "down payment" on **much, much more** that God has reserved for your inheritance.

Ephesians 1:14 in the King James Version uses the word *earnest.* When a person purchases a house, he puts **"earnest money"** down on it. That cash is a pledge of the full amount due, to be paid at a future time when he takes the house as his personal possession.

What a striking illustration of **salvation future!** The "earnest" of your "inheritance" has already been paid: You have the Holy Spirit. One day Christ will take you to Himself. He will redeem His purchased possession. And when He does, your salvation will be complete.

Now read carefully 1 Peter 1:3-5. Do these verses speak of your **salvation past** or your **salvation future?**

    ❏ A. Salvation past   ❏ C. Both past and future
    ❏ B. Salvation future   ❏ D. Neither past nor future

The correct answer, of course, is that these verses refer **both** to that which Christ has already done for you (salvation past) **and** to that part of your salvation that is still in the future. As you read your Bible in the years ahead, you will find many passages of Scripture like this one. Be alert to the **three aspects of salvation!**

Look next at 1 Peter 1:6-9. Which of the three aspects of salvation do you see in these verses?

    ❏ A. Salvation past   ❏ C. Salvation future
    ❏ B. Salvation present   ❏ D. All of these

Do you agree that **D** is the best answer? First Peter 1:6-9 refers to your faith in Jesus Christ, whom you have never seen with your physical eyes. This relates to **salvation past.** It also refers to the trials you are going through now, which serve to prove the genuineness of your faith. This relates to **salvation present.** And it further refers to a coming day when the testing of your faith will result in praise and glory and honor. This relates to **salvation future.**

Verses 7 and 13 of 1 Peter 1 even tell you the exact time when you will be given your future salvation. When is it?

_____

At the **revelation** or **revealing** or **appearing** of Jesus Christ, you will receive your promised inheritance. *In your Quiet Time, be sure to thank God for His promise of salvation future.*

How is your daily Quiet Time developing? It has been about 40 days since you began using your SURVIVAL KIT. *Circle the approximate number of days you have had a meaningful time of Bible study and prayer.*

1 2 3 4 5 6 7 8 9 10 11 12 13 14 15 16 17 18 19 20 21 22

23 24 25 26 27 28 29 30 31 32 33 34 35 36 37 38 39 40

WEEK 6: THREE ASPECTS OF SALVATION—PART ONE: ITS BEGINNING AND COMPLETION
DAY 5: FREE FROM THE OLD NATURE

Read Romans 5:12; 6:23; 1 Corinthians 15:50-57; 2 Corinthians 5:1-9. Quote from memory Psalm 119:11; Romans 12:4-5; 1 Peter 4:10; Galatians 5:22-23; Colossians 3:8-10; and Philippians 1:6.

SALVATION FUTURE! What will salvation provide for you that you do not have now and that you will not have until Christ comes again? The Bible tells of your future inheritance.

Read Romans 5:12 and Romans 6:23. What two short, grim, fatal words are connected in both of these verses? _____ and

_____.

What is the relationship between **sin** and **death,** according to Romans 6:23?

_____

_____

WILL YOU EVER BE RID OF THAT OLD NATURE, THE NATURE OF SIN? **YES!** Because of sin, death awaits every person. Only those who are alive when Christ comes will not know its sting. But a time is coming when you will be set free from the **presence of the old nature.**

Read now one of the most striking passages the apostle Paul ever wrote: 1 Corinthians 15:50-57. Write verse numbers as indicated.

A. Which verses tell you that your future salvation will come at a **point in time?**

A. _____

B. Which verses connect **death** with **sin?**

B. _____

C. Which verse tells you that you cannot inherit the kingdom of God with the **old nature** still within you?

C. _____

D. Which verses assure you that you are guaranteed **immortality,** as the old nature will be removed?

D. _____

E. Which verse assures you that this is the work of **Jesus Christ,** not the result of your own "good deeds"?

E. _____

(Answers: A-51-52, B-55-56, C-50, D-53-54, E-57)

Consider now the teaching in 2 Corinthians 5:1-9. Verse 1 describes our lives as though they were **"houses"** or **"tents."** Verses 2-4 describe us as **"groaning"** in our present "house." In your opinion, which of the following answers best describes the reason for our groaning?

❑ A. Christians have such hard times in this present life.
❑ B. Christians are terrified of dying.
❑ C. Christians desire to be set free from the old nature.

Verses 2 and 4 make the right answer clear, don't they? In verse 8 the apostle Paul plainly said he had rather cast aside his body with its **human nature,** so as to be "at home with the Lord" (2 Corinthians 5:8, NASB).

Write here the verses that you have learned about putting off the old nature.

_____

_____

_____

_____ (Colossians 3:8-10).

Read Romans 5:6-11. Memorize Romans 5:10.

Review the **three aspects** of salvation.

SALVATION PAST   By the **blood of Christ,** you are forever set free from the **penalty** of sin.

SALVATION FUTURE   By the **return of Christ,** you will be forever set free from the **presence** of sin.

SALVATION PRESENT Through the **indwelling life of Christ,** you are here and now set free from the **power** of sin!

Christ has given you, **right now,** freedom from the **power** of sin. *Study Romans 5:6-9.* Which aspect of salvation do these verses speak of? In the middle of which verse does the thought pattern pass from **salvation past** to **salvation future?** _____

_____

Romans 5:6-8 describes the greatness of God's love for sinners in sending Christ to die for us. This description of **salvation past** continues in **verse 9** with the statement that "we are now justified by his blood" (Romans 5:9, RSV). In the **middle of that verse,** the emphasis shifts to **salvation future,** when we shall be saved from any further judgment of God.

Romans 5:10 also begins by speaking of **salvation past:** "We were God's enemies, but he made us his friends through the death of his Son" (Romans 5:10, GNB). Then the verse moves on to speak of which aspect of salvation?

_____

According to Romans 5:10, who is the **source** of our **salvation present?**

_____

Can you use the same verse to complete the following sentence? By **Christ's death,** I have received **salvation past;** now through **Christs** _____

_____, I daily receive **salvation** _____.

Through **Christ's life,** you daily receive **salvation present.**

Salvation present means that you can "exult in God." The word *exult* means **"to leap about; to be extremely joyful."** *Can you list three things in your personal life that Christ has brought you—things that make you want to "exult in God"?*

1. _____

2. _____

3. _____

Whatever you wrote, whatever makes you joyful as a Christian, never forget who brings these joys into your life. Romans 5:10 is a key verse to understanding **salvation present,** which you enjoy now because of the **indwelling Christ, controlling all.**

WEEK 7: THREE ASPECTS OF SALVATION— PART TWO: A DAILY PROCESS
DAY 2: SAVED BY HIS LIFE

Read Hebrews 2:14-15,18; 4:14-16.

"SAVED BY HIS LIFE"–**Salvation present** is the result of your Lord Jesus Christ living in you. He provides His mighty power to set you free from the power of sin.

But . . . does He really understand your needs, your weaknesses, your temptations? Today's Scripture passages can help you realize that He does!

Read Hebrews 4:14-16. These verses picture Jesus in a way the Jewish people, or Hebrews, could understand easily. In their religion they had a **high priest** who went into the sanctuary and offered sacrifices so that sins could be forgiven. The writer of Hebrews described Jesus as **what kind** of high priest who has gone into **where?**

_____   _____

Jesus is our **great** High Priest, who has gone into the **heavens**—that is, "into the very presence of God" (Hebrews 4:14, GNB). According to verse 15, **how** does this great High Priest feel about the temptations to sin which you encounter, and **why** does He feel this way about them?

_____

_____

_____

_____

Jesus **sympathizes** with you; He is **touched by your weaknesses.** Why? Because He Himself has been **"tempted in every way that we are"** (Hebrews 4:15, GNB). But note the crucial difference between Jesus and everyone else who has ever lived: **"yet without sin"** (Hebrews 4:15, RSV).

According to Hebrews 4:16, what are you able to do because of Jesus' sympathy with your temptations to sin?

_____

_____

Stop right now and go boldly, confidently to God's throne of grace. Ask God for the strength you need to resist temptation. After your prayer, read Hebrews 2:14-15,18. According to the first part of verse 14, what did Jesus do so that He might understand you perfectly?

_____

_____

Jesus **took part** in your **human nature;** He **shared** the **same flesh and blood** that you do. To what length did Jesus go in order to experience personally every single thing that you as a human being must endure? One stark, five-letter word in the middle of verse 14 gives you the answer.

_____

_____

In addition to becoming flesh and blood and enduring all that you might have to endure in life, Jesus actually shared the human experience of **death!** Therefore, there is nothing in all your life span that He has not faced personally.

Read Ephesians 5:18. Quote from memory Romans 5:10.

The indwelling Christ brings victory into every part of your life. He was tested in every way you might be but did not sin. He will not permit you to be tempted beyond your capacity. He will always give you a way to escape.

He not only **protects** you; He also provides all the resources you need! *Read Ephesians 5:18.*

It is important to know two things about the Greek word used in the original text of Ephesians 5:18, which is translated **"be filled"**:
1. It is a verb form expressing **continued action:** "be being filled."
2. It is an **imperative** verb—an order, a command.

So you see this is not an optional feature of the Christian life:

YOU ARE ORDERED TO BE CONTINUALLY FILLED WITH THE SPIRIT.

Ephesians 5:18 commands you to be **filled continually** with the Spirit of Christ. This aspect of **salvation present** as a **daily process** should remind you that you are saved not only by the **death** of Christ, but also by the _____ of Christ. *Can you write here Romans 5:10, your Scripture memory verse that states this great truth?*

_____

_____

_____

_____

_____

Salvation present is guaranteed by Christ! He offers you an unending supply of His Spirit. Whenever you are thirsty, you need only come to Him and **drink.** The result will be Christ's Spirit filling your personality with His life. When that has happened, others will recognize quickly that you are more than yourself. **"Rivers of living water"** will flow out from your life and bless the lives of others.

Are you thirsty? Come to Christ and **drink!**

WEEK 7: THREE ASPECTS OF SALVATION—PART TWO: A DAILY PROCESS
DAY 4: WORKING OUT WHAT GOD IS WORKING IN

Read Philippians 2:5-13; Hebrews 13:20-21.

Christ the Son of God understands everything you face in your daily life. He experienced it all for your sake.

One of the clearest statements of this truth in all the Bible is found in Philippians 2:5-8. *Read those verses now.* (It may help you to know that v. 6 could be reworded this way: "Christ Jesus was in the form of God but did not think of equality with God as something He must hold on to.") What two words in verse 7 tell you Jesus was willing to experience **anything** you may experience in life?

_____   _____

Did you write **"servant"** or **"slave"** in one of those blanks? Did you write

"men" or **"human"** in the other blank? What word, used twice in verse 8, tells you how far Jesus was willing to go to share the common experience of humanity?

_____

Because of Jesus' voluntary sacrificial **death,** what has God done? *Read Philippians 2:9-11; then summarize in your own words what God has done.*

_____

_____

Here's one way to summarize Philippians 2:9-11: **"God has made Jesus higher than all and will cause all to confess that fact."** Specifically, what is "every tongue" to confess, according to verse 11?

_____

Now read Philippians 2:12-13. Do those verses seem a bit odd or out of place, coming right after God has made every tongue confess that **"Jesus Christ is Lord"**? Immediately after you are told that God has exalted Christ (who lives in you) to be the King of kings and the Lord of lords, immediately after you are told that every knee must bow before Him, . . . then you are told to "work out your own salvation with fear and trembling" (Philippians 2:12). What a strange thing to say!

But look again at Philippians 2:12. Why are you to work out your salvation present **"with fear and trembling"**? Certainly **not** because you are afraid of being punished by an angry God! No, it must mean something else. Here's what it is: You **fear** missing God's blessing in your life. And you **tremble** to think of living your life without His presence being fully in charge of your personality.

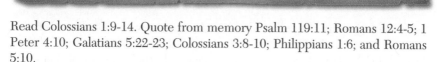

WEEK 7: THREE ASPECTS OF SALVATION—
PART TWO: A DAILY PROCESS
DAY 5: SALVATION IS RESCUE

Read Colossians 1:9-14. Quote from memory Psalm 119:11; Romans 12:4-5; 1 Peter 4:10; Galatians 5:22-23; Colossians 3:8-10; Philippians 1:6; and Romans 5:10.

It should be obvious to you by now that God **has** performed, **is** performing, and **will** perform the actions of salvation in your life. Salvation begins at a

point in time, with confession of your sin and confession of Christ's lordship. It continues as a **process of time,** in which you are freed from sin's power by Christ's indwelling life. In a final **future** event Christ will liberate you from the old nature of sin within your life.

Read Colossians 1:9-14. Which of these verses describes **salvation past?** Which describes **salvation present?** Which describes **salvation future?**

Colossians 1:10-11   **Colossians 1:12**   **Colossians 1:13-14**

Salvation past: _____

Salvation present: _____

Salvation future: _____

(**You should have written the references in this order: 13-14; 10-11; 12.**)

In Colossians 1:9, the apostle Paul said he was praying for a very important kind of **knowledge.** What kind was it?

_____

God wants you, too, to "be filled with the **knowledge of His will.**" He wants you to understand how His salvation comes to you in three aspects—**past, present,** and **future.** He wants you to know the certainty of your **salvation past,** wrought by Christ's death on the cross. He wants you to feel the assurance of your **salvation present,** as Christ's saving life gives you strength to resist temptations to sin. One very important truth has been saved until last in our study of the three aspects of salvation: Exactly what is **"salvation"?**

Imagine you are standing on the shore of a lake. You see a man in the middle of the water. He is unable to keep himself afloat. He will soon die if someone doesn't save him! What is the **element** that will kill him? **Water.** He will drown in **water.** To be "saved," he must be taken from the **water.**

Salvation is leaving the self-owned life and receiving the Christ-owned life. SALVATION IS GOD'S ACT OF RESCUING YOU FROM A SELF-DIRECTED LIFE. First, at a point in time, He took you out of that state. Next, as a daily process, He makes it possible for you to live a Christ-directed life. Finally, in a future event, He will set you free permanently from the **possibility** of a self-owned life. That is **salvation.**

Read Colossians 2:1-4,8,20-23. Memorize 1 Corinthians 2:14.

"I want to see somebody with a little **authority** around here!" How many times have you heard or said words like those? Nobody likes to deal with those who can do only as they're told. Everybody sometimes feels a need to get to whoever or whatever is the final **authority.** This week you will study three subtle and dangerous sources of authority. Next week you will concentrate on the one true source of authority. *Study the chart which summarizes the four sources of authority. Write each above the description that you think it best fits.*

Read Colossians 2:1-4. In verse 2, Paul said that he desired **wealth** for the Colossian Christians; what kind of wealth did he mean?

A _____ OF U _____

In his desire that the Colossian Christians would have full **assurance** of **understanding,** Paul told them that in **"Christ Himself"** they would find all the treasures of _____ and _____

Why did Paul want his fellow believers to know the treasures of **wisdom** and **knowledge** hidden in Christ? Verse 4 tells you.

_____

Lest you be **deceived** or **deluded** or **beguiled** by inadequate sources of authority, you need to know what Paul wrote in Colossians 2:8.

How many **inadequate sources of authority** did Paul mention in Colossians 2:8? *Write here words from that verse that refer to each of them.*

INTELLECT: _____

TRADITION: _____

EXPERIENCES: _____

Your Scripture memory selection for this week explains how a person can be taken captive by falsehood. Look at 1 Corinthians 2:14. Tomorrow you will study this verse in more detail. *Begin now to memorize it.*

God gave you your mind, your **intellect;** He expects you to use it. God gives you **experiences,** and these may be most meaningful. Some things are unchanging, regardless of passing centuries; some **traditions**—especially those based on the Scriptures—are worth preserving. But neither intellect, nor experiences, nor tradition should become **ultimate authority** for faith!

EXPERIENCE   INTELLECT   SCRIPTURE   TRADITION

SOURCES INSIDE MAN HIMSELF	SOURCES OUTSIDE MAN
man determines truth by his ability to reason what is right or wrong, good or bad and so on.	man structures beliefs which have been important to his ancestors.
man determines truth by his senses, feelings and emotions.	God reveals truth in written form; knowledge is ultimate and complete.

You should have arranged the titles on the chart like this:

INTELLECT	TRADITION
EXPERIENCES	SCRIPTURE

WEEK 8: FOUR SOURCES OF AUTHORITY–PART ONE: THREE INADEQUATE SOURCES
DAY 2: INTELLECT! REASON! LOGIC!

Read 1 Corinthians 1:18-25; 2:7-14.

Many people are determined to make their **intellect** the final authority in all matters. "If it seems **logical** to me, I shall believe it!" In no other way does man more clearly crown **himself** "god" of his life. He has the egotism to believe that his own intelligence is capable of making final judgments about truth and error, good and evil, right or wrong.

The apostle Paul had to cope with people who had made **intellect** the source of authority for their beliefs. *Read 1 Corinthians 1:18-25.* Trying to **debate** or **dispute** with anyone about what he believes rarely does any good. In fact, Paul even said (in v. 20) that God has made **foolish** all the W _____

_____ of the W_____.

Paul analyzed the way two ethnic groups of his day used the wisdom of the world: "Jews want miracles for proof, and Greeks look for wisdom. As for us, we proclaim the crucified Christ, a message that is offensive to the Jews and nonsense to the Gentiles; but for those whom God has called, both Jews and Gentiles, this message is Christ, who is the power of God and the wisdom of God. For what seems to be God's foolishness is wiser than human wisdom, and what seems to be God's weakness is stronger than human strength" (1 Corinthians 1:22-25, GNB).

Not that the Christian faith is anti-intellectual—far from it! The apostle Paul himself had one of the most brilliant and highly educated minds of his century. *Read 1 Corinthians 2:7-8 to learn* **what kind** *of wisdom Paul taught.* He said that if earthly rulers had understood this **true** wisdom, they would not have committed what terrible crime?

65

_____

No, Paul did not accuse humanity of having too much wisdom but rather, too little. If they had had enough true wisdom, they would not have **crucified the Lord Jesus Christ.** *Now read 1 Corinthians 2:9-11 to learn why people of the world did not understand who Jesus was and why He came.* According to verse 11, who is the only person that understands God's thoughts?

_____

If only **the Spirit of God** understands the thoughts of God, what is the only way anyone else can understand them? **"We as Christians have received the Spirit of God, who teaches us God's truth."** According to 1 Corinthians 2:14, why is it impossible for a person to find God through his own intellect?

_____

The **natural, worldly** person (and that means anyone who has not committed his life to Christ) **has not received the Spirit of God.** According to that same verse, can you reason with an unbeliever and thus bring him to faith by the authority of intellect?

No, when speaking with a person who holds to intellect as **ultimate authority,** you cannot depend on reason alone. You must ask God to use His Holy Spirit to create the kind of awareness and conviction that will prepare such a person to believe.

You should have found 1 Corinthians 2:14 familiar when you read it today. *Try reciting it from memory.*

WEEK 8: FOUR SOURCES OF AUTHORITY—PART ONE: THREE INADEQUATE SOURCES DAY 3: EXPERIENCES! VISIONS! IMPRESSIONS!

Read Deuteronomy 13:1-4; Colossians 2:18-19. Quote from memory 1 Corinthians 2:14.

From the beginning of time, people have founded religions on the various **experiences** they have had. Making experiences their authority, they have called upon others to share these experiences. A person who has not had such experiences must be "initiated" into them or be considered inferior, spiritually substandard.

The problem of evaluating truth in an experience is a very serious matter. If someone tells you he has had a vision sent from God, how can you be certain that what he is saying is true? Authority based on experiences is a most dangerous thing. That is why God has found a better way to reveal Himself to man. He has given us a written record of truth. By it, you can judge all the many experiences that people claim come from God.

You can find a good example of this in Deuteronomy, the fifth book of the Bible. *Read Deuteronomy 13:1-4.* According to these verses, which is a sure test of truth in the experience of a prophet or a dreamer?

❑ A. Whether the prophecy or dream comes true.
❑ B. Whether the prophet or dreamer entices you to turn away from the one true God.

The teaching is clear. Even when someone can show you signs and wonders, even when his predictions seem accurate, you must not listen to him **if he lessens your singlehearted devotion to God.** Deuteronomy 13:3 explains **why** those who make **experiences** their religious authority sometimes seem so persuasive. What reason does that verse give?

God may use a prophet, a dreamer, or a miracle-worker **to test the sincerity of your love for Him.** But He will not let the testing become too hard for you.

Now think again about problems caused by those who cling to **experiences** as the source of religious authority. *Read Colossians 2:18-19.* What specific problem was the apostle Paul writing about?

_____

_____

Some of the Colossians apparently had experienced **visions.** As a result, they were trying to make all the Christians join them in **worship of angels** and in other false religious practices. According to verse 19, what mistake is made by people who use **experiences** as their authority?

_____

The apostle Paul made a strong statement about those who lean on experiences as their authority: **They do not hold fast to Christ, the Head** of His body, the church. Experiences do not tend to cement people together in a church. Instead, they tend to cause divisions. Those who have had a certain experience tend to look down on those who have not. But Christ does not emphasize "experiences"; He supplies you with **His own life.** This is what causes **"a growth which is from God"** (Colossians 2:19, NASB).

Be sensitive to those who encourage you to seek an experience. When God gives you a special time of fellowship, it can be a blessing to all. But when you begin to seek the **experience** rather than the **fellowship with God,** watch out. You may be "captured" by a false source of authority!

WEEK 8: FOUR SOURCES OF AUTHORITY—PART ONE: THREE INADEQUATE SOURCES
DAY 4: TRADITION!

Read Matthew 15:1-9.

"It's a **tradition!**" "We've **always** done it this way!" "We must not **change!**"

How do traditions develop? Someone in the past decided that a particular teaching or custom or ceremony should be repeated again and again. For that person, the teaching or custom or ceremony was extremely important. It had to be preserved.

Often, however, the deep **heart-meaning** of the teaching or custom or ceremony is lost. Only the **form** remains. It is observed as a dead ritual, bringing no help to people. Furthermore, it calls for no real **heart commitment. Tradition** can become a jail cell, imprisoning people who might find the true meaning of the original teaching or custom or ceremony if it were expressed in some other way.

Read Matthew 15:1-9. Why were the religious leaders of Jesus' day (the Pharisees and the scribes) critical of Jesus' disciples?

_____

_____

Jesus' disciples broke with **tradition** by **failing to wash their hands** in a certain customary way **before eating bread.** But Jesus replied that these religious leaders themselves were ignoring a more important matter. Which of the Ten Commandments did He accuse them of breaking?

_____

The Pharisees and the scribes were breaking (or at least "bending"!) the Commandment **"Honor your father and mother."** In Matthew 15:6, **which two** of the four sources of religious authority does Jesus mention as clashing with each other?

_____ VERSUS _____

When it comes to **Scripture versus tradition,** you as a Christian must make a clear-cut choice. *Summarize in your own words the prophecy of Isaiah quoted by Jesus in Matthew 15:8-9.*

_____

_____

Some people **give God lip service instead of heart service.** They **substitute man-made doctrines for God-given truths.**

According to 1 Peter 1:18-19, can **tradition** bring salvation to people? In light of the verses from Matthew which you have studied today, why not?

_____

_____

Did you write that tradition tends to become a matter of **outward expression,** not of the **heart,** and that **human traditions** sometimes actually **clash with God's Word?**

WEEK 8: FOUR SOURCES OF AUTHORITY—PART ONE: THREE INADEQUATE SOURCES DAY 5: INTELLECT! EXPERIENCES! TRADITION!

69

Read 1 Timothy 1:3-7; 6:20-21; 2 Timothy 2:15-19. Quote from memory Psalm 119:11; Romans 12:4-5; 1 Peter 4:10; Galatians 5:22-23; Colossians 3:8-10; Philippians 1:6; Romans 5:10; and 1 Corinthians 2:14.

As a new Christian, you will be exposed to many types of religious teaching. Many sincere, earnest people will present to you their systems of belief. Examine them carefully. Are they based on **intellect?** MAN'S MIND CAN-NOT BE THE FINAL JUDGE OF TRUTH. Are they based on **experiences?** MAN'S ACTIVITIES CANNOT BECOME THE FINAL SOURCE OF TRUTH. Are they based on **tradition?** MAN'S PAST INTELLECT AND EXPERIENCES ARE NO MORE TRUSTWORTHY THAN HIS PRESENT ONES!

Read 1 Timothy 1:3-7. According to verse 4, what do man-made teachings lead to?

_____

Mere **speculations** or **questions** or **arguments** do nothing to strengthen you as a Christian. On the other hand, what does true teaching from God lead to? *(See v. 5.)* _____

_____

First Timothy 1:5 in the *Good News Bible* speaks of **"the love that comes from a pure heart, a clear conscience, and a genuine faith"** (GNB).

What **impure** personal motives do false teachers have, according to verse 7?

_____

"Teachers of the law" in New Testament times were people in places of honor. And there are still people today who want to get honor and glory by teaching inadequate sources of authority! *Read 1 Timothy 6:20-21.* What did the apostle Paul instruct his young assistant Timothy to do with the truth he had been given from God? _____

_____

If Timothy **guarded** and **kept safe** the true teaching, how was he to react to false teachers? _____

Paul warned young Timothy to **shun** or to **avoid** false and foolish ideas. Second Timothy 2:15-19 contains further instructions from Paul to Timothy. Which of the **four sources of authority** is mentioned in verse 15?

_____

But Hymenaeus and Philetus turned away from **the Scriptures** to another source of authority. Based on verses 16-18, which one do you think it was?

_____

Apparently **intellect** was the inadequate source of authority used by these two false teachers. According to verses 18-19, their teachings **upset the faith of some people;** but the **firm foundation** of teachings from the **Word of God stood** as strong as ever (2 Timothy 2:18-19).

It is only during this week that you have used your SURVIVAL KIT to study the **four sources of authority.** But you have been learning from the very beginning that **Scripture** is your authority as a Christian. What Scripture verse have you learned that tells what Christ has done for you, by His **life** and by His **death?** *Write here Romans 5:10.*

_____

_____

_____

Read 2 Timothy 1:1-2,5; 3:14-17. Memorize 2 Timothy 3:16.

Four sources of authority . . . but only one of them is trustworthy! The apostle Paul knew which one that was. *Read 2 Timothy 3:14-17.*

Having studied the Scriptures **ever since he was a child,** Timothy knew they were able to give him what? _____ This wisdom leads to **"salvation through faith in Jesus Christ."**

Focus now on 2 Timothy 3:14. What did the apostle Paul instruct young Timothy to continue in?

_____

What is the difference between **learning** a truth and **firmly believing** that truth?

_____

Firm belief in what you are taught comes more easily when **the people who teach you also exemplify those teachings** in their lives. Verse 14 says that Timothy knew who his teachers were. Do you? *Find three of them in 2 Timothy 1:1-2,5; write here their names and relationships to Timothy.*

_____, who was Timothy's _____

_____, who was Timothy's _____

_____, who was Timothy's _____

No doubt you listed **Lois,** who was Timothy's **grandmother,** and **Eunice,** who was Timothy's **mother.** What relationship did you list for **Paul?** In verse 2 Paul called Timothy his son, but he was using that word in a figurative sense. Timothy's father was apparently dead or otherwise removed from the household in which the boy grew up. Because of this situation and because Paul had become like Timothy's **spiritual father,** Paul referred to him as "my dearly beloved son."

Focus now on 2 Timothy 3:16. Who inspired the Scriptures? _____

_____

Because **God** inspired the Bible, what is it useful for?

_____   _____

_____   _____

If you study the Scriptures, which are useful for **"teaching the truth, rebuking error, correcting faults,** and **giving instruction for right living,"** obviously this will have an effect on your life. *Focus now on verse 17.* What will you become as you study the Scriptures?

_____

_____

Do you really want to become **"fully qualified and equipped to do every kind of good deed"?** If you do, you know how. You are doing it now if you are being faithful in reading the Bible during your daily Quiet Time, working through the study guides in your SURVIVAL KIT, and learning your Scripture memory verses. Do you still remember your first memory assignment—a verse explaining why it is so important to memorize God's Word? *Recall Psalm 119:11.*

Timothy had been studying the Scriptures from the time he was a child. You cannot begin your own lifetime of study any sooner than **today!** Make a commitment in prayer now: For the rest of your life, will you give priority time to reading God's Holy Scriptures?

WEEK 9: FOUR SOURCES OF AUTHORITY— PART TWO: ONE TRUE SOURCE DAY 2: SCRIPTURE BEFORE EXPERIENCE

Read 2 Peter 1:16-21; Matthew 17:1-5.

You have read many passages of Scripture written by the apostle **Paul.** You have found these passages in books of the Bible grouped in the section called **Paul's Letters.** Right after that section comes another section of New Testament books called **General Letters.** Two of those inspired books were written by the apostle **Peter.**

Read 2 Peter 1:16-18. In this passage, Peter referred to a remarkable event which he had witnessed personally. That event was the **transfiguration** of Jesus Christ. *Read these statements Peter made about it* (quoted here from the **Revised Standard Version of the Bible**).

_____ "We were eyewitnesses of his majesty."

_____ "He received honor and glory from God the Father."

_____ "The voice was borne to him . . ., 'This is my beloved Son, with whom I am well pleased.' "

_____ "We heard this voice borne from heaven."

_____ "We were with him on the holy mountain."

Now read in Matthew 17:1-5 the actual account of this event. In front of each statement made by the apostle Peter in later years (above), write the number of a matching verse from Matthew 17:1-5. (Some verses may be used more than once.) See how closely Peter's statements match what actually happened.

You should have listed verse numbers from Matthew 17 in this order:
2, 5, 5, 5, 1

73

It's clear that Peter knew what he was talking about, isn't it? He actually stood on the mountain of transfiguration and saw Jesus glorified. He heard the voice of God the Father from heaven. In 2 Peter 1:16, Peter stated his personal knowledge that this event in the life of Jesus Christ was **not** a **"cleverly devised tale."** It really happened, and Peter was personally present to see it happen!

Read carefully what Peter said next in 2 Peter 1:19-21. Do you notice that he spoke of something being **"made more sure"**? What could be more sure than something that he had witnessed in person? You might say, "Nothing could be any more sure than that!" Yet Peter said, "So we are **even more confident** of the message proclaimed by the prophets" (2 Peter 1:19, GNB). In other words, Peter was saying: "There **is** something even more trustworthy than what I saw and heard myself—namely, the words written by men who were guided by the Holy Spirit of God!"

In 2 Peter 1:20-21, the apostle Peter made two important **negative** statements about the things written in the Holy Scriptures. *In your own words, write here what Peter said the Bible is not.*

1. The Bible is **not** _____

2. The Bible is **not** _____

Peter stated that the Bible is **not a private or individual interpretation of truth.** Nor is it **the result of an act of the human will.** Rather, it is the result of the activity of **God.** GOD BREATHED UPON MEN AS THEY RECORDED GOD'S TRUTH.

What principle can you set up for your own life as a result of Peter's teaching in this passage—a principle related to your **final authority** for matters of faith? *Pray about this question during your Quiet Time.*

WEEK 9: FOUR SOURCES OF AUTHORITY— PART TWO: ONE TRUE SOURCE DAY 3: AN AMAZING BOOK

Read Micah 5:2; Matthew 2:1-6; 27:13-14,38,57-60; Isaiah 53:5,7,9; John 14:2-3; 19:1,4,34; 20:25. Quote from memory 2 Timothy 3:16.

An amazing book, the Bible! In it are hundreds of statements about events that had not happened when the authors wrote about them. Prophecies about future kings and kingdoms, predictions of births and deaths, forecasts of the coming of the Savior into the world—all these are found in the pages of the Bible.

For example, read Micah 5:2; then read Matthew 2:1-6. Where did the prophet Micah say the Savior was to be born? _____

Where was Jesus born? _____

In about 740 B.C. the prophet Micah predicted that Jesus would be born in Bethlehem. Mary, Jesus' mother, lived in Nazareth. Because of an order from the Roman government, she had to travel to Bethlehem and was there when Jesus was born. At the time that Mary conceived, even she could not have guessed that this would happen. *Read next a part of a marvelous prophetic poem: Isaiah 53:5,7,9.* This quotation from the **New American Standard Bible** is divided properly into poetic lines, which have been marked here as subdivisions of the verses (such as 5*a*, 7*b*, and so on).

5*a* He was pierced through for our transgressions,
5*b* He was crushed for our iniquities;
5*c* The chastening for our well-being fell upon Him,
5*d* And by His scourging we are healed.
7*a* He was oppressed and He was afflicted,
7*b* Yet He did not open His mouth.
9*a* His grave was assigned to be with wicked men,
9*b* Yet with a rich man in His death;
9*c* Although He had done no violence,
9*d* Nor was there any deceit in His mouth (Isaiah 53:5,7*ab*,9, NASB).

Read now the New Testament verses listed below. Beside each one, write the number and letter of one or more verse subdivisions from Isaiah 53 (such as 5a or 9c). See how accurately the prophet predicted facts about Jesus' trial, suffering, crucifixion, death, and burial!

_____ John 19:34   _____ Matthew 27:14

_____ John 20:25   _____ Matthew 27:38

_____ John 19:1   _____ Matthew 27:57-60

_____ Matthew 27:13   _____ John 19:4

Look below (and right side up) to see how you should have matched Isaiah 53 with New Testament verses:

9c, 9d John 19:4
9b   Matthew 27:57-60
9a   Matthew 27:38
7b   Matthew 27:14

7a   Matthew 27:13
5d   John 19:1
5a   John 20:25
5a   John 19:34

Many biblical prophecies already have come true. This is why you can be confident that the **others eventually will be fulfilled** as well.

Read Psalms 19:7-11; 37:29-31; 119:89-91,98-101.

What does the **Bible itself** say about the Bible?

It says that the Bible is **an eternal source of wisdom and righteousness.**

Before opening your Bible, read these two explanations: (1) In the verses to be studied today, you will find many different expressions for the Word of God, such as **law, precepts, testimonies, statutes, commandments, judgments.** (2) The expression **"Word of God,"** as used in the Bible, has a broader meaning than the Bible alone. It means **anything God says about Himself,** whether through the voice of His prophet or through the majesty of His creation or through the ordering of human history in His world. "The Word of God" means the **active expression of God's very nature.** As such, it certainly **includes** the Scriptures—those **writings** that are the unique record of God's activity.

Now read carefully each of the verses listed at the top of this page. These verses focus on three great claims the Bible makes for itself: that it is **eternal** or **everlasting,** that it is **a source of wisdom,** and that it is **a source of righteousness.** *Beside each of the following key words, write the reference for each verse you read in which the Bible makes that claim for itself.*

ETERNAL: _____

WISDOM: _____

RIGHTEOUSNESS: _____

Do your completed lists look like these?
  ETERNAL: Psalms 19:9; 119:89-91
  WISDOM: Psalms 19:7; 119:98-100
  RIGHTEOUSNESS: Psalms 19:8-9,11; 37:29-31; 119:101

In addition to the verses you have read today, you also have been learning another passage in which the Bible makes statements about itself. Can you quote it? (2 Timothy 3:16).
Another verse which you have learned explains why many people misunderstand the Bible. The Bible was **inspired** by the Spirit of God and can be **interpreted rightly** only by people who are **indwelled** by the Spirit of God. *Quote a verse stating this fact (1 Corinthians 2:14).*

WEEK 9: FOUR SOURCES OF AUTHORITY— PART TWO: ONE TRUE SOURCE
DAY 5: FOUR SOURCES OF AUTHORITY? OR ONE?

Read 1 Corinthians 15:3-7; Acts 18:24. Quote from memory Psalm 119:11; Romans 12:4-5; 1 Peter 4:10; Galatians 5:22-23; Colossians 3:8-10; Philippians 1:6; Romans 5:10; 1 Corinthians 2:14; and 2 Timothy 3:16.

Four sources of authority . . . but only **one** of them is trustworthy. You know which one that is.

The apostle Paul also knew which source of authority is trustworthy. *Read what Paul wrote in 1 Corinthians 15:3-7.* Twice Paul mentioned the authority he was using for his summary of the death, burial, and resurrection of Jesus Christ. Which source of authority was it? _____

_____

Can **you** use the same authority Paul used when sharing Christ's life with others?

                    Yes _____ No _____

Yes, you also can use the **Scriptures** as your source of authority when sharing Christ's life with others. But this doesn't "just come naturally" to you as a Christian. *Read in Acts 18:24,28 a capsule biography of a Christian named Apollos.* How do you think Apollos became so skilled in his knowledge and use of the Scriptures?

_____

_____

_____

Is it important to **you** to know the Scriptures as well as Apollos knew them? Is it important enough to rearrange your own personal priorities in order to **study the Scriptures** as Apollos must have studied them? What areas of your life might have to be "rearranged" to provide the needed time for a lifetime habit of daily Bible study?

_____

_____

_____

_____

_____

In all honesty, are you ready and willing to do that rearranging at this time?

Yes _____   No _____

During these nine weeks, you already have looked at dozens of Bible verses. When you have completed your SURVIVAL KIT, **don't break the habit of personal Bible study!** If you will continue to use this same time **daily** for the rest of your life, you will soon become an "Apollos"!

Within the body of Christ, you will find those who have a special ability to put the deepest knowledge about the Bible into words. Cultivate friendship with them. They will **bless your life!** But at the same time, don't forget: **Study** the Word. **Memorize** the Word. **Meditate** on the Word. From it, **all your future growth** as a Christian will develop!

Read Philippians 4:6 and memorize it.

Look at your left hand. Use the fingers on that hand to count five people, presently in your life, who will not permit you to share your new faith with them. They are cold, even scoffing, toward your life in Christ. You have a great desire to share your new life with them so that they may also enjoy it. But they will not even listen to you talk about Jesus Christ.

What can you do? PRAY FOR THEM!

Look at your right hand. Count on those fingers five people presently in your life who will permit you to share your new faith with them. Although they are not ready to place their lives in Christ's control, they are curious about the change they observe in you.

What can you do? WITNESS TO THEM!

Next week your Bible study will focus on **witnessing.** But the power of **prayer** is even more important than witnessing because it can work with both those who **will** and those who **will not** let you share Christ with them. A great Christian once said: "You can do **more** than pray, **after** you have prayed. BUT YOU CAN DO NO MORE THAN PRAY—UNTIL YOU HAVE PRAYED!"

Look now at Philippians 4:6. If you are using the **King James Version,** read **"anxious"** in place of the word *careful.* According to this verse, what is the alternative to being **anxious** about any situation you face in life?

_____

What **limits** does this verse place on the things you can **pray about?**

_____

As a Christian you can **talk to God in prayer about everything.** What is prayer, anyway? Nothing more than **letting Christ use His power to work in an area of need**—in your life or in the life of another. Prayer is your invitation to Christ to come into that area of need. The answer to your prayer does not depend on your power in prayer but on **His** power to work in that area of need. Therefore, praying for your unbelieving friends who will **not** permit you to share Christ with them is simply **inviting Christ to work in their lives in spite of their attitude toward you.**

Use the chart to make personal preparation for using the Five-and Five Principle in your life as a Christian. In the left column, thoughtfully list the names of five people who presently will not permit you to share your faith with them. In the right column, prayerfully list the names of five people who will permit you to talk with them about your new life in Jesus Christ.

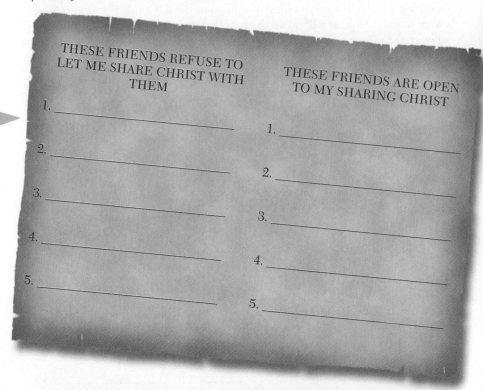

THESE FRIENDS REFUSE TO LET ME SHARE CHRIST WITH THEM

1. _____

2. _____

3. _____

4. _____

5. _____

THESE FRIENDS ARE OPEN TO MY SHARING CHRIST

1. _____

2. _____

3. _____

4. _____

5. _____

WEEK 10: THE FIVE-AND-FIVE PRINCIPLE—FIVE YOU CAN WIN BY PRAYER
DAY 2: A LITTLE FAITH IS ENOUGH!

Read Matthew 17:20; 21:21-22; James 1:5-8; John 6:37.

Read Matthew 21:21-22 and James 1:5-8. As you think about praying for the salvation of your friends, do the verses you have just read tend to discourage you or even to fill you with despair? They probably do! *Write here the fear you feel, related to your praying for others.*

_____

_____

Perhaps you have written words like these: **If my faith isn't strong enough, I won't get any answers to my prayers. So, prayer is not for me; I'm honest enough to admit I have a weak faith.**

Add another Scripture verse to those above: *Read the words of Jesus in John 6:37:* "The one who comes to Me I will certainly not cast out" (NASB). **How much faith** do you need to have before Jesus will answer your prayers? Jesus said that even a faith as small as a mustard seed is enough! *(If you don't believe that, read Matthew 17:20.)* If your faith is able to bring you to Jesus with your need, it is enough! He has promised that He will honor such faith. He will **"certainly not cast out"** anyone who trusts Him.

If you have enough faith to come to Jesus with your inability to help yourself, He will deal with your **doubts.** Don't feel your faith is so weak it would do no good to pray. **Remember:** PRAYER IS SIMPLY LETTING CHRIST USE HIS POWER TO WORK IN AN AREA OF NEED—IN YOUR LIFE OR IN THE LIFE OF ANOTHER.

If your faith in Jesus is **just large enough** to **ask** Him to use His power and to reveal Himself to your **Five-and-Five** people, then it's large enough. The greatest faith in the world is the one that admits its limits and then tells Jesus you are leaving everything to Him. So, don't be afraid you will **limit** His power by your faith. PRAY! It is no more complicated than giving your Lord access to an area of need. Just let yourself go in your prayer times, as Philippians 4:6 encourages you to do. (Have you memorized that verse yet?) *Write it here.*

_____

_____

_____

The only way you will **ever** discover the power of prayer in reaching the "unreachables" in your life is to **pray** for them. *Today think of each of the Five-and-Five you listed yesterday.* One by one, turn them over to Jesus. Pray about a specific area of need in each life. Invite Jesus to enter that area of need with

His power. Then wait for the results of your praying. God has His own timetable for answering . . . and **answer He will!**

WEEK 10: THE FIVE-AND-FIVE PRINCIPLE—FIVE YOU CAN WIN BY PRAYER
DAY 3: THREE ASPECTS OF PRAYER

Read Matthew 7:7-11. Quote from memory Philippians 4:6.

The three aspects of **salvation** have to do with **past, present,** and **future.** Not so the three aspects of **prayer,** because all of them have to do with your **present fellowship with God.** What memory verse assures you it is **useful** or **profitable** to have **daily fellowship with God through His Word?**

_____

_____

_____

_____

_____(2 Timothy 3:16).

Now read Matthew 7:7-8. Often we describe praying as the **action** of **"talking with God."** These verses from Matthew describe praying as **three actions.** In the three verbs used, you can see **three aspects of prayer.** *List below these three actions. Then write beside each of them God's response to that action.*

ACTION	RESPONSE
1. _____	_____
2. _____	_____
3. _____	_____

Meditate on the three verbs or action words used in Matthew 7:7-8.

Asking involves requesting something that you already know about: "Lord Jesus, I ask You to bring my friend **to know Your love.**" You already know about Christ's love; you simply want it to be known by your unbelieving friend.

82

Seeking, on the other hand, involves requesting an answer about something you do **not** know about: "Lord Jesus, show me what I can do to express Your love to my friend. I don't know what to do next!"

Knocking involves asking Christ to enter an area of need that is behind closed doors: "Lord Jesus, misbehavior in my friend's life has closed him to Your life. Open the door to that area of need in him and show him how You can deliver him."

Read Matthew 7:9-11. These verses make several comparisons. Which comparison is most important?

_____

The most important comparison in Matthew 7:9-11 does not involve bread or stone, a fish or a snake. Rather, it is the comparison of **human fathers'** integrity and compassion with that of your **Heavenly Father.** What assurance do these verses give you that your **asking, seeking,** and **knocking** in prayer will be answered?

_____

_____

If **human fathers** give what their children ask for, how much more likely is it that our **Heavenly Father** will give what we ask for!

WEEK 10: THE FIVE-AND-FIVE PRINCIPLE—FIVE YOU CAN WIN BY PRAYER
DAY 4: PRAYER IS IMPORTANT!

Read Matthew 14:23; Mark 1:35; Luke 6:12; 22:39-41.

The apostle Paul knew that **prayer is important.** *Write here something Paul once said that proves he knew prayer is important.*

_____

_____

_____

_____

_____ (Philippians 4:6).

Now read Matthew 14:23; Mark 1:35; Luke 6:12; and Luke 22:39-41. According to these verses, **where** did Jesus go to pray? *You should be able to list three places.*

1. _____

                                    3. _____

2. _____

What times of day did Jesus choose for His prayer times? *You should be able to list two times.*

1. _____   2. _____

Jesus prayed **in the hills, at a lonely or solitary place,** and **on the Mount of Olives.** He prayed **at night** and **at early morning before daybreak.** In your opinion, **why** did Jesus choose such times and places for prayer?

_____

Sometimes Jesus found a solitary place where He could communicate with His Heavenly Father.

Luke 22:41 should have given you a clue in answering that last question. Jesus withdrew "about a stone's throw" from His disciples (Luke 22:41, NASB). He chose **times and places when He could be alone with God** the Father.

Luke 6:12 tells you that Jesus sometimes **prayed the whole night through.** *Think what this means:* Jesus lived in constant prayer fellowship with God the Father. Nevertheless, He found it necessary to withdraw from the pressures of life, at regular times and at special places, in order to pray. Sometimes He even prayed for hours at a time. If the Lord Jesus found it necessary to make a habit of prayer, **how about you?** Would **you** also profit from doing so?

Look at your left hand. Think about the **Five-and-Five Principle.** What would happen if you spent in **prayer** for your five **"unreachable"** friends the time you would **like** to spend witnessing to them or studying the Bible with them?

WEEK 10: THE FIVE-AND-FIVE PRINCIPLE—FIVE YOU CAN WIN BY PRAYER
DAY 5: PRAYER BRINGS POWER TO WIN

Read John 14:13-14; Matthew 28:18-20. Quote from memory Psalm 119:11; Romans 12:4-5; 1 Peter 4:10; Galatians 5:22-23; Colossians 3:8-10; Philippians 1:6; Romans 5:10; 1 Corinthians 2:14; 2 Timothy 3:16; and Philippians 4:6.

Are you already putting the **Five-and-Five Principle** to work in your life? Are you praying specifically for five people who will **not** let you share Christ with them? Are you **asking, seeking,** and **knocking** in your prayers as you invite Christ into their areas of need?

Read what Jesus said in John 14:13-14. Each of those verses tells you to ask in a certain way as you pray. The instructions are given twice.

You are to make your requests **in the name of** _____. When you make your requests in the name of **Jesus,** whose glorious power is released to work? _____

God the Father, who is **all-powerful,** will be **glorified in Christ the Son** as you pray in Jesus' name. *Now read Matthew 28:18-20.* According to verse 18, **how much power** is released by praying in the name of Jesus?

_____

"All power is given unto Me in heaven and in earth." What an awesome statement! And what an awesome power is at your disposal through praying **in Jesus' name!**

(Here's a helpful hint: Matthew 28:18-20 will be the memory selection you should start learning at the beginning of next week. It is also the longest assignment for memorization you have been given in your SURVIVAL KIT. Since that is true, get a good start working on it over the weekend. You'll be glad you did!)

Learn a lesson of the **Five-and-Five Principle.** Have you decided during this week that it is easier to pray for the five who are **open** to your sharing than for the five who are **closed** to it? Perhaps you think those you can **only** pray for will be the last to come to receive Christ as Savior and Lord because they are the hardest to reach.

ARE THEY? You must reject the idea that the five on your left hand are harder for Christ to reach than the five on your right hand! What you think is "hard" and "easy" looks completely different to God. Such conclusions on your part only hinder your prayer life. When you pray **in the name of Jesus** for these friends, the One you are inviting to enter their lives has all power **in heaven and on earth.**

If a cyclone is sweeping through a forest, does it matter whether some of the trees are hardwood and others softwood? Of course not! The cyclone's power is so overwhelmingly greater than either softwood or hardwood that it makes no difference whatever.

Saul of Tarsus was a powerful, murderous opponent of Christianity. No one could witness directly to him. He was hateful and destructive to Christians. Yet, **the power of Christ** used Stephen's death to bring Saul to salvation.

Do not underestimate the power of your prayers for the five who are hard and rejecting. When you ask the Lord to enter a life through **asking, seeking,** and **knocking,** never doubt His ability to do what you ask. He can do more than you ask or think! In **His name** rests all the power there is in the entire universe.

Read Matthew 28:18-20 and memorize it.

FIVE YOU CAN WIN THROUGH PRAYER ALONE!
FIVE YOU CAN WIN THROUGH SHARING YOUR WITNESS!
That's the **Five-and-Five Principle.**

For the rest of your life, keep the 10 fingers of your two hands full. As long as you serve Christ, always have **five people** you are **praying for** and **five people** you are **witnessing to.** You will find that witnessing to five and praying for five others at the same time is a full-time job for a believer!

The word *witness* translates a Greek word, *maturia.* Do you see the English word *martyr* in it? Many of those who first shared their witness for Christ died for doing so, thus giving that meaning to "martyr." The basic meaning of the word, however, is **one who furnishes evidence.**

Witnessing is not preaching. It is not even teaching the Bible. It is **giving evidence.** You have come to believe in Christ as your Savior and Lord. As a result, He lives in your life. You have prayed continually for His Spirit to fill you. As a result, your personality has an "added ingredient." It is evident to others who are near you. **You are a witness** because you are bearing evidence to those who live around you. It's not so much something **you do** as it is the natural result of Christ living in you and flowing His love through you.

Shortly before Jesus left this earth (in bodily form) and returned to His heavenly glory, He stated to His followers a **great claim,** a **great command,** and a **great promise.** All three of these are found in **Matthew 28:18-20,** your new memory selection. Since you were given a helpful hint toward the end of last week, you already may be able to write it here from memory. *Try to do so now. If you can't do that yet, copy it carefully from whatever translation you are using for memorization.*

87

_____

_____

_____

_____

_____

_____

_____

_____

Now mark an X in the margin of this page beside the great claim that Jesus stated in Matthew 28:18-20. You studied this claim last week as you were learning about the great **power** of prayer.

If you found the **great claim** Jesus stated in the first part of Matthew 28:18-20, you should be able to find the **great promise** Jesus stated in the last part of those same verses. Everything in between is the **great command** that Jesus gave to all His followers. Sometimes it is called **"The Great Commission."**

WEEK 11: THE FIVE-AND-FIVE PRINCIPLE—FIVE YOU CAN WIN BY WITNESSING DAY 2: CHRIST EMPOWERS YOUR WITNESS

Read Ephesians 5:18; Acts 2:1-18.

Since beginning to use this SURVIVAL KIT, you have memorized many passages about the **Holy Spirit.** *Read Ephesians 5:18. Next read Acts 2:13-18.* What **comparison** is made in both of these passages?

_____

Both Ephesians 5:18 and Acts 2:13-18 compare **drinking wine** with **being filled with the Holy Spirit.** *Now read the whole story in Acts 2:1-18.* What was the **essential ingredient** in the witness of those Christians?

_____

Did you write that the **filling of the Holy Spirit** was the essential ingredient? *Now read carefully the two statements below. Think again about Acts 2:1-18.* Mark which statement is correct.

- ❑ The Holy Spirit simply gave those people a new **inner experience** and did not expect them to verbalize it; it was enough for them to bear a **"silent witness."**
- ❑ The first act of the Holy Spirit, upon filling those people, was to make it possible for them to **speak their witness** to unbelievers so that every single person there would **hear** about Christ.

What is the result of a person's **being filled with the Spirit of Christ?**

_____

The result is **speaking, not silence!** For you as a person controlled by the **indwelling Christ,** what will witnessing involve?

- ❑ Living for Christ without speaking about Christ.
- ❑ Speaking about Christ without living for Christ.
- ❑ Both living for Christ and speaking about Christ.

Someone has said, "The greatest hypocrite in the world is the one who says, 'I don't have to **talk** to others about Christ; all they have to do is observe my actions, and they will know I am a Christian.' " Good old Ego! How it loves to **protect** itself against exposure. But when Self is no longer king and Christ reigns, then you will speak of Him.

"But," you say, "what is there in **my** life that would be important to an unbeliever? I know only a few basics about the Christian life. I must wait until I know more about the Scriptures to witness."

NOT SO!

You have already passed from death to life. Christ's Spirit already lives in you and fills you constantly on request. **Remember: A witness is one who gives evidence.** You have much to give evidence about as Christ lives through you.

Your five friends are open to your sharing. They are curious. Don't be afraid! Talk about what has happened in your life. Share the daily pilgrimage with Christ that you are now experiencing. Share it in conversation with the five who are open to your testimony. DO IT TODAY.

Read Romans 1:16; Acts 22:1-15; 26:9-20. Quote from memory Matthew 28:18-20.

You have the evidence of a **changed life**, of **the indwelling Christ, controlling all.** You need to **verbalize** that witness, to tell people who Christ is and what He has done and how much He means to you now.

The apostle Paul knew how to **verbalize his witness.** Furthermore, he did so at every opportunity, to everyone who would listen. *Read aloud these words that Paul once wrote:* "I am not ashamed of the gospel of Christ: for it is the power of God unto salvation to every one that believeth." Can you honestly make the same statement Paul made in **Romans 1:16?**

At least twice in the Scriptures you may find detailed records of times when Paul verbalized his witness. *Read now Acts 22:1-15 and Acts 26:9-20.* Notice that in each case Paul used **his own conversion experience** as the **evidence** he gave in witnessing. In both instances, he mentioned **four things** about it. These four things are listed and numbered in the following chart. In Acts 22:1-15 and in Acts 26:9-20 Paul verbalized his witness about these four things in the **same order** they are numbered here.

PAUL'S CONVERSION EXPERIENCE	ACTS 22	ACTS 26
1. Paul had not always followed Christ.	vv. 3-5	vv. 9-12
2. God began to deal with Paul's rebellion.		
3. Paul received Christ as his Lord.		
4. Paul's new life was centered on Christ's purposes.		

In the proper column, write the references of two to four consecutive verses from Acts 22 in which Paul told about each of four parts of his conversion experience. Then follow the same instructions with that other recorded time when Paul verbalized his witness, in Acts 26. (**Remember:** You should be able to find each of these four in **not less than two nor more than four verses in**

a row. And all of these groupings of two to four verses each will come **in order, as listed on the chart.** The first one in each column has already been filled in for you.)

KEY	
ACTS 22	**ACTS 26**
vv. 3-5	vv. 9-12
vv. 6-9	vv. 13-18
vv. 10-13	v. 19
vv. 14-15	vv. 19-20

You will be amazed to discover that most unbelievers have **never heard anyone** share information of the type Paul shared in verbalizing his witness! Every conversion experience is different from all others. Therefore, your own testimony of how you came to know Christ is **personal** and **individual.** It is **evidence** that no one but you can give. No one else will ever duplicate it.

WEEK 11: THE FIVE-AND-FIVE PRINCIPLE—FIVE YOU CAN WIN BY WITNESSING
DAY 4: THE PERSONAL TOUCH

Read Matthew 9:10-13; 1 Corinthians 9:19-23.

It probably hasn't been too long since you became a Christian. As you considered giving your life to Christ, what—or **who**—had a great influence on you?

_____

Now read Matthew 9:10-11. What criticism did people make of Jesus?

_____

Why do you suppose Jesus risked criticism by having **personal contact with evil people?** *Read Matthew 9:12-13 before answering.*

_____

Jesus came to **call sinners to repentance.** He had **mercy** or **compassion** on those who were **spiritually sick.** *Now read what the apostle Paul wrote in 1 Corinthians 9:19-21.* Which of these is what Paul meant?

- ❏ A. "It doesn't matter to me who I associate with."
- ❏ B. "I agree with whoever I happen to be with at the time."
- ❏ C. "I deliberately cultivate the friendship of all sorts of people."

Sentence **C** fairly states Paul's approach to making friends. **Why** did Paul feel such a philosophy of life was necessary? *Read 1 Corinthians 9:22-23 before answering.*

Paul did it all **for the sake of the gospel, the good news.** A realist if there ever was one, Paul knew that not everyone whose friendship he cultivated would accept Christ. But he was willing to associate with anyone and everyone so that he "might **by all means save some**" (1 Corinthians 9:22). He knew that **God's power would save anyone who believed.**

Interestingly enough, Acts does not give a single instance where a person came to know Christ without the aid of a Christian! Christ sent Peter to a Roman soldier. He sent Philip to an Ethiopian official. He sent Paul to Lydia and her friends, to the jailer at Philippi, and to many others. IN EVERY CASE, A PERSONAL TOUCH WAS PROVIDED.

Look again at your right hand. Those five people are **open** to your sharing with them. You should give **time** to them! Share your life with them. They have few other sources that they can turn to where the **river of love** is flowing. As you share your life with them, they will see Christ in your words, in your life, and in your thoughts. Such exposure to the Christ who dwells in you will have a tremendous impact on them.

Once again, **priorities** need to be kept straight! *Take another look at your weekly schedule.* Is there **time** for those five people? If not, what can be put **lower** on your schedule of priorities to make room for them? *Pray about your answer during your daily Quiet Time.*

Look now at your left hand. Are you still remembering to pray for those five people who at present are **not** open to your witness?

Read Matthew 18:19-20; Acts 2:41-47. Quote from memory Psalm 119:11; Romans 12:4-5; 1 Peter 4:10; Galatians 5:22-23; Colossians 3:8-10; Philippians 1:6; Romans 5:10; 1 Corinthians 2:14; 2 Timothy 3:16; Philippians 4:6; and Matthew 28:18-20.

Most things about the Christian life are better **caught** than **taught.** *Read Matthew 18:19-20.* Verse 20 speaks of **how many people being gathered together** in the name of Christ? _____ Verse 19 contains what great **prayer promise** made by Jesus?

_____

_____

Where even **two or three people gather** in Jesus' name, **He promises to be with them.** When **two people agree** on a request to be prayed for in Jesus' name, **He promises to grant it.** What does this mean to you, as you look at your two hands and think of those **five-and-five** people who do not yet know Jesus Christ as Lord and Savior? Has someone come into your life who is a more mature Christian than you are—someone with whom you could **join in prayer** for salvation of your **five-and-five?**

Yes _____ No _____ If so, who? _____

Remember: Most things about the Christian life are better **caught** than **taught.** Your growth as a Christian will be strengthened as you associate with others who have had a longer time to grow than you have. *Read now some verses you read several weeks ago when you studied about the one body of Christ, the church: Acts 2:41-47.* Those early Christians didn't try to "go it alone," did they? They shared everything they had; they shared their very lives with their fellow believers in the body of Christ.

FIVE FOR WHOM YOU PRAY!
FIVE TO WHOM YOU WITNESS!

In your wildest imagination, can you imagine what an impact would be made on the world if **every Christian** were to commit time to reaching 10 people constantly, using this Five-and-Five Principle?

Your journey has just begun. The Scripture passages you have studied, the verses you have memorized—these are only the beginning of your learning; there will be **much more** for you to discover about your inheritance, your rights and privileges as a child of God. From those of us who are your older brothers and sisters in the body, another hearty greeting:

"WELCOME, FRIEND! ENTER WITH US INTO ALL CHRIST HAS RESERVED FOR US . . . **TOGETHER.**"

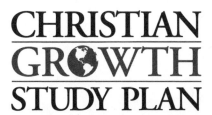

CHRISTIAN GROWTH STUDY PLAN

Preparing Christians to Serve

In the **Christian Growth Study Plan (formerly Church Study Course),** this book *Survival Kit for Youth* is a resource for course credit in the subject area Personal Life of the Christian Growth category of plans. To receive credit, read the book, complete the learning activities, show your work to your pastor, a staff member or church leader, then complete the information on the next page. This page may be duplicated. Send the completed page to:

**Christian Growth Study Plan, One LifeWay Plaza,
Nashville, TN 37234-0117, FAX: (615)251-5067.
E-mail: cgspnet@lifeway.com**

For information about the Christian Growth Study Plan, refer to the current Christian Growth Study Plan Catalog. It is located online at *www.lifeway.com/cgsp*. If you do not have access to the Internet, contact the Christian Growth Study Plan office, (1.800.968.5519) for the specific plan you need for your ministry.

SURVIVAL KIT FOR YOUTH
CG-0410

PARTICIPANT INFORMATION

Social Security Number (USA ONLY-optional)
— — —

Personal CGSP Number*
— —

Name (First, Middle, Last)

Home Phone
—

Date of Birth (MONTH, DAY, YEAR)
— —

Address (Street, Route, or P.O. Box)

City, State, or Province

Zip/Postal Code

Please check appropriate box: ☐ Resource purchased by self ☐ Resource purchased by church ☐ Other

CHURCH INFORMATION

Church Name

Address (Street, Route, or P.O. Box)

City, State, or Province

Zip/Postal Code

CHANGE REQUEST ONLY

☐ Former Name

☐ Former Address

City, State, or Province

Zip/Postal Code

☐ Former Church

City, State, or Province

Zip/Postal Code

Signature of Pastor, Conference Leader, or Other Church Leader

Date

*New participants are requested but not required to give SS# and date of birth. Existing participants, please give CGSP# when using SS# for the first time. Thereafter, only one ID# is required. **Mail to:** Christian Growth Study Plan, One LifeWay Plaza, Nashville, TN 37234-0117. Fax: (615)251-5067.

Rev. 3-03